# Acknowledgements

*Deep South Knitting* will always have a special place in my heart since it has been a true family affair. Many members of my family and my friends provided hands-on help and even more were loudly cheerleading from the sidelines. Thanks to all of them for believing in me and for sharing my excitement along the way.

There are some very special people who made this venture possible that I want to thank individually. First, my fabulous husband, Michael Langan, who is, as I like to remind him, my favorite husband *so far*. Michael supported the decision to ditch my law career for something I loved. He offered me not just moral support, but financial support as well. Some days I don't deserve you, my love, but we both know that most days you're darn lucky to have me. This book is for you.

Next, I must thank my darling and brilliant niece, Erin Janes Brooks, who programmed and designed my original website as a gift. That little online yarn shop directory grew into something more than I could have imagined— Planet Purl. And though she rolls her eyes and denies it, my writing a knitting book was her idea. Her design genius is also largely responsible for the beautiful look of this book. Erin, words are insufficient to thank you for helping me craft my new life as well as crafting this project. A huge kiss to you, sweet girl, for turning the book in my head into the book in my hands.

My son, Cavan, a talented, funny, amazing actor and singer and even more amazing writer, contributed his editing skills for the non-technical portions of the book and made my writing so much smarter. He also flew home to serve as production assistant for most of our photo shoot, working as a second pair of hands in the kitchen as I Tasmanian-deviled my way through three marathon days of cooking and baking every goody in this book. Cavan good-naturedly submitted to posing for the Ozark Vest. Yes, I totally took advantage of you, and I love you for always humoring me. You really are the world's best son.

Two of our beautiful models are my baby sister, Patricia Short, and her daughter, Olivia. I had so much fun shopping for styling stuff with you two. I love you both and am grateful to have such good-looking relatives.

I would also like to thank some folks who, though not related by blood, are part of my *Deep South Knitting* family. My friend and former knitting student, Elisha Charpentier graciously agreed to model. Thank you for helping showcase our designs. Thanks to my intrepid test knitters, Mary Ann Cruse and Cindy Thorn, who kept me on track to get projects knit, or re-knit, in time for scheduled shooting. Special thanks to our technical editor, Amy Polcyn, herself a fab designer and published author, for being my second (and much more focused) pair of eyes. Thanks to my friend, Deborah Nelson, who sat across the kitchen table from me for hours as we proofread out loud. And of course, thanks to the many friends and fans of PlanetPurl.com for their loyal support.

Last, but not least, I'd like to thank *you* for buying this book. Thank you for being part of my dream and I hope you enjoy!

# Table of Contents

## Patterns

*Knitting, traveling and cooking with a Southern accent*

Beth Moriarty

Book Design: Erin Janes Brooks
Text Editor: Cavan Hallman
Technical Editor: Amy Polcyn
Project Photography: Bev Brosius
Graphics Design: Jamie Dennis
Jewelry courtesy KittensVintage.com

**Planet Purl Press**
PO Box 149524
Orlando, FL 32814, USA
www.PlanetPurl.com

Printed in China through Asia Pacific Offset

Library of Congress Cataloging-in-Publication Data

Moriarty, Beth, 1956-
Deep South Knitting: Knitting, Traveling and Cooking with a Southern Accent/ Beth Moriarty

1st ed. - Planet Purl Press, 2011.

156 p. : illus. ; 22cm - (Knitting patterns, travel in US South, southern regional cooking). - Includes index.

ISBN 978-0-615-52854-0 (pbk.)

Library of Congress Control Number: 2011915633

## Southern Recipes



## Extras

*For Michael,*
*who never tells me I have*
*too much yarn.*

# Welcome

Although I was born in Chicago, I've lived south of the Mason-Dixon Line most of my life. Despite the fact my parents are New Yorkers, as were their parents, and that I grew up in coastal Florida, not a quintessentially "Southern" location, I identify myself as a Southern woman. I think this started when I went to college in Mississippi, sharing a dorm with girls who thought *I* spoke with an accent. When my parents dropped me off for my freshman year and drove away, they waved goodbye and my father called out the window, "Bye, Peaches!" The family joke was that I needed a new nickname if I were going to fit in with my new college's bevy of belles and cotillion-ready debutantes. The joke was on my parents when they phoned a week later and didn't even recognize my voice— I was already speaking with a Southern accent! Decades later, that drawl still occasionally sneaks out, especially when I'm happy or excited.

I only lived in Mississippi for a year, and then Georgia for another year, but the South became such a part of me that no matter where I lived over the next 30 years, I always *felt* Southern. When the discussion started at Planet Purl about doing a regional-themed knitting book, the South was a natural first choice.

This collection features 16 of my own designs, inspired by the history, native plants, architecture and flowers (lots of flowers), that define "Southern" for me. We are fortunate to have contributions from 9 other Deep South designers who have created projects inspired by their hometowns. To make these patterns accessible for knitters and crocheters of all experience levels, I've recorded how-to videos for every skill needed to complete the projects in this book; you can find them on PlanetPurl.com.

If you can't make it down to our neck of the woods for a visit, doing a little Southern cooking of your own might just be the next best thing. I've included a dozen of my favorite regional recipes to give you a true "taste" of the South. So put on the kettle, get comfy and plan to stay awhile. Welcome to my neighborhood— welcome to *Deep South Knitting*.

DWARE
ED COAL HARNESSES
CAL
US
No 1

Nowhere else in the country were the sharp divisions of the Civil War experienced as they were in West Virginia. When abolitionist John Brown seized an arsenal in Harpers Ferry with the intention of arming the slaves of northern Virginia, the state's secessionists were sent into a panic. The majority of the Virginia Convention voted to join the Confederacy. However, the vast majority of delegates from the state's western region voted against secession. The westerners decided that independent statehood was the only solution and after years of debate, President Lincoln issued a proclamation of statehood for West Virginia in 1863.

West Virginia is the vacation destination in the East for outdoor enthusiasts. The only state that is completely within a mountain range, it boasts world class whitewater rafting, hunting, fishing, horseback trails and mountain biking and hiking over hundreds of miles of paths. In the winter, downhill and cross-country skiers, snowboarders and snowtubers flock to the state.

West Virginia's beautiful state parks are due in large part to the Civilian Conservation Corps, part of FDR's "New Deal." Many forests were clear-cut during the Great Depression by landowners desperate for income. Fifty-five thousand West Virginia men went to work in 65 mountain camps, replanting trees and building recreation facilities. The tree nursery at Camp Parsons alone was responsible for growing 7.5 million replanted trees. Many of these facilities remain, reminders of a time when the preservation and restoration of our country's natural beauty was a national priority.

For a look at what West Virginians are made of, visit Eleanor or Arthurdale, two towns built under Roosevelt to relocate displaced mine and farm families on emergency relief. The families built homes, worked subsistence farms, created co-operative stores and ran their own schools. These towns stand as testaments to West Virginia's indomitable spirit.

# 1865 Jacket

## Harpers Ferry, West Virginia

*West Virginia's Civil War history is unique in that the state itself was born from the conflict between North and South. Virginia and West Virginia were one unified state, but when residents of the western region allied with Union troops, the Virginia Commonwealth was split. Union troops set fire to the arsenal at Harpers Ferry, and the war began.*

*This lightweight, feminine version of a denim jacket celebrates the joining of Union Blue and Dixie Gray. It has a beautiful drape that allows the fabric to breathe and is knit in a cotton/lempur blend yarn making it more fluid and forgiving of minor tension fluctuations than the average cotton. The lacy collar and split sleeves are inspired by traditional styles of the mid-19th century. Toss it on over a tee and jeans for a softer take on denim casual, or wear it with linen pants and a silk tank for a spring or summer evening out.*

## About this Project

**Skill Level:** Intermediate

**Finished Sizes:** XXS (XS, S, M, L, XL, 1X, 2X) with finished bust sizes 38 (39, 41, 42, 43, 45, 46, 48)" [96.5 (99, 104, 107, 109, 114, 117, 122)cm]

**Fit Tip:** This jacket is fitted, but body-skimming, and designed to be worn with about 3-4" (7.5-10cm) of ease. Choose a finished size 3-4" (7.5-10cm) larger than your bust measurement. Elisha is wearing a size XS.

**Project Gauge:** 20 stitches and 26 rows = 4" (10cm) in stockinette stitch

### Shopping List

Louisa Harding *Albero* (50% cotton, 50% lempur/viscose, 110 yards/100m); 9 (10, 10, 11, 11, 12, 12, 13) skeins Denim #11 and 5 (5, 6, 6, 6, 6, 7, 7) skeins Dove #03

Size US 7 (4.5mm) needles

Size US H-8 (5.00mm) crochet hook

Size US F-5 (3.75mm) crochet hook

Tapestry needle

One 3/4" (8mm) button

## Instructions

*Back*

With Denim, CO 90 (92, 94, 96, 98, 100, 104, 108) stitches. Knit one row. Using knitted cast on, CO 6 (7, 7, 8, 9, 10, 10, 11) stitches at the beginning of each of the next two rows. [102 (106, 108, 112, 116, 120, 124, 130) stitches]. Work even in stockinette stitch for 7 (7, 7, 9, 9, 11, 11, 11) rows, ending with a WS row. [10 (10, 10, 12, 12, 14, 14, 14) rows worked].

*Waist decrease row (worked on RS)*: K1, ssk, knit to last three stitches, ssk, k1. (One stitch decreased at each edge). Repeat *waist decrease row* every other RS row 6 (5, 4, 3, 1, 1, 0, 0) time(s), then every third RS row 2 (3, 4, 5, 7, 6, 7, 7) times. [84 (88, 90, 94, 98, 104, 108, 114) stitches]. Work even for 15 (15, 15, 13, 11, 17, 17, 19) rows, ending with a WS row. [62 (64, 66, 68, 70, 72, 74, 76) rows worked].

*Waist increase row (worked on RS)*: K1, m1, knit to last three stitches, m1, k1. (One stitch increased at each edge). Repeat *waist increase row* every third RS row 1 (0, 1, 0, 1, 0, 0, 0) time(s), then every fourth RS row 4 (0, 4, 3, 1, 1, 3, 0) time(s), then every fifth RS row 0 (4, 0, 1, 2, 2, 0, 2) time(s). [96 (98, 102, 104, 108, 112, 116, 120) stitches]. Work even for 3 (1, 1, 3, 3, 7, 9, 11) row(s), ending with a WS row. [104 (106, 106, 106, 108, 108, 108, 108) rows worked].

*Shape armholes*

BO 5 (5, 3, 2, 5, 3, 5, 6) stitches at beginning of next two rows. Then BO 2 (2, 4, 5, 3, 6, 5, 5) stitches at the beginning of each of the next two rows. [82 (84, 88, 90, 92, 94, 96, 98) stitches]. Work even for 0 (0, 0, 2, 2, 0, 0, 0) rows, ending with a WS row.

*Armhole decrease row (worked on RS)*: K1, ssk, knit to last three stitches, ssk, k1. (One stitch decreased at each edge). Repeat *armhole decrease row* every RS row 3 (2, 4, 4, 5, 6, 5, 5) times, then every third RS row 1 (3, 2, 2, 2, 1, 3, 3) time(s). [72 (72, 74, 76, 76, 78, 78, 80) stitches]. Work even for 31 (21, 25, 27, 25, 31, 23, 27) rows. [152 (154, 156, 160, 162, 162, 164, 168) rows worked].

*Shape shoulders and back neck*

Mark center 10 (10, 10, 10, 12, 12, 14, 14) stitches. BO 6 (7, 6, 7, 6, 1, 2, 5) stitch(es) at beginning of each of the next two rows.

*Size 1X only*: Work even 2 rows.

*Sizes L, XL, 1X, 2X only*:

BO 5 stitches at the beginning of each of the next two rows.

*All sizes*:

Center neck bind off: BO 7 (6, 6, 6, 5, 5, 5, 5) stitches. Knit to marked center neck stitches. Join second ball of yarn and BO 10 (10, 10, 10, 12, 12, 14, 14) center neck stitches. Knit to end. Work both shoulders at the same time from this point.

The entire town of Harpers Ferry is designated a National Historic Park. The story of our country can be told here, beginning with George Washington and Thomas Jefferson through John Brown's raid and the founding of the NAACP.

Next row (WS): BO 7 (6, 6, 6, 5, 5, 5, 5) stitches at first shoulder edge, purl to neck edge. BO 9 (0, 0, 0, 8, 8, 6, 4) stitches at neck edge of second shoulder, purl to end.
Next row (RS): BO 9 (0, 0, 6, 0, 6, 6, 5) stitches at first shoulder edge, knit to neck edge. BO 9 (9, 5, 4, 8, 8, 6, 4) stitches at neck edge of second shoulder, knit to end.
Next row (WS): BO 9 (0, 5, 6, 0, 6, 6, 5) stitches at first shoulder edge, purl to neck edge. BO 0 (9, 5, 4, 0, 0, 0, 4) stitches at neck edge of second shoulder, purl to end.
*Note*: Size XXS completed at this point.
Next row (RS): BO 0 (9, 10, 10, 8, 8, 8, 0) stitches at first shoulder edge, knit to neck edge. BO 0 (9, 10, 10, 8, 8, 8, 4) stitches at neck edge of second shoulder, knit to end.
*Note*: Sizes XS, S, M, L, XL, 1X completed at this point.
*Size 2X only*:
Next row (WS): BO remaining stitches.

*Front left*
With Denim, CO 45 (46, 47, 48, 49, 50, 52, 54) stitches. Knit one row. Purl one row. Using knitted cast on, CO 6 (7, 7, 8, 9, 10, 10, 11) stitches at the beginning of the next row (outside hip). [51 (53, 54, 56, 58, 60, 62, 65) stitches]. Work even in stockinette stitch for 7 (7, 7, 9, 9, 11, 11, 11) rows, ending with a WS row. [10 (10, 10, 12, 12, 14, 14, 14) rows worked].
*Waist decrease row (worked on RS)*: K1, ssk, knit to end. (One stitch decreased at hip edge).
Repeat *waist decrease row* every other RS row 5 (5, 2, 3, 1, 1, 0, 0) time(s), then every third RS row 3 (3, 6, 5, 7, 6, 7, 7) times. [42 (44, 45, 47, 49, 52, 54, 57) stitches]. Work even for 13 (15, 11, 13, 11, 17, 17, 21) rows, ending with a WS row. [62 (64, 66, 68, 70, 72, 74, 76) rows worked].
*Waist increase row (worked on RS)*: K1, m1, knit to last three stitches, m1, k1. (One stitch increased at waist edge).
Repeat *waist increase row* every third RS row 1 (1, 1, 0, 4, 0, 0, 0) time(s), then every fourth RS row 2 (1, 2, 1, 0, 1, 2, 0), time(s), then every fifth RS row 0 (0, 0, 1, 0, 1, 0, 2) time(s). [46 (47, 49, 50, 54, 55, 57, 60) stitches]. Work even for 3 (11, 3, 5, 1, 5, 7, 0) row(s), ending with a WS row. [88 (90, 92, 92, 96, 96, 98, 100) rows worked].
*Begin front neck shaping*
Decrease one stitch at neck edge. Repeat neck edge decrease every RS row 3 (1, 2, 2, 3, 3, 2, 3) time(s), then every other RS row 2 (3, 2, 2, 1, 1, 1, 0) time(s).
**At same time** continue *waist increase row* every other RS row 1 (1, 1, 1, 1, 1, 1, 0) time(s), then every fourth RS row 1 (1, 0, 1, 0, 0, 0, 0) time(s).
Work even for 1 row. [42 (44, 45, 47, 50, 51, 54, 56) stitches and 104 (106, 106, 106, 108, 108, 108, 108) rows worked].
*Begin armhole shaping/continue neck shaping*
BO 5 stitches at side edge. Work even 1 row. BO an additional 2 (2, 2, 2, 3, 3, 4, 5) stitches at side edge. Work even 1 row.
*Size M, L, XL, 1X, 2X only:*
Work one additional BO row, binding off 2 stitches. Work one row even.
*Sizes L, XL, 1X, 2X only:*
Work a second additional BO row, binding off 2 stitches. Work one row even.
*All sizes*:
Decrease one stitch at neck edge and armhole edge. Work one row even.
Repeat neck edge decrease every other RS row 3 (1, 5, 4, 6, 2, 1, 0) time(s), then every third RS row 2 (4, 1, 0, 0, 4, 6, 2) time(s), and then every fourth RS rows 2 (2, 3, 4, 3, 1, 1, 5) time(s).
**At same time** repeat armhole decrease every RS row 3 (3, 3, 2, 2, 2, 2, 3) times, then every other RS row 0 (1, 1, 2, 2, 2, 2, 3) time(s), then every third RS row 1 (0, 0, 0, 1, 0, 1, 1) time(s), and then every fourth RS row 0 (2, 2, 0, 0, 0, 0, 0) times.
When neck and armhole decreases are completed, work even 1 row. [22 (22, 22, 24, 24, 25, 26, 26) stitches remain and 150 (156, 158, 162, 164, 164, 166, 170) rows have been worked].
*Shoulder shaping*
*Sizes XXS (XS, S) only*:
BO 6 (6, 6) stitches at armhole edge. Work even 1 row. BO an additional 7 (6, 6) stitches at armhole edge. Work even 4 (1, 1) row(s). BO remaining 9 (9, 10) stitches.
*Sizes M (L, XL) only*:
BO 2 (6, 6) stitches at armhole edge. Work even 1 row. BO an additional 6 (5, 6) stitches at armhole edge. Work even one row. On next row, BO additional 6 (5, 5) stitches at armhole edge. Work even 1 row. BO remaining 10 (8, 8) stitches.
*Size 1X only*:
BO 2 stitches at armhole edge. Work even 1 row. BO an additional 5 stitches at armhole edge and decrease 1 stitch at neck edge. Work even one row. On next row, BO additional 5 stitches at armhole edge and decrease 1 stitch at neck edge. Work 1 row. BO remaining 6 stitches.
*Size 2X only*:
BO 5 stitches at armhole edge. Work even 1 row. BO an additional 5 stitches at armhole edge and decrease 1 stitch at

neck edge. Work even one row. *On next row, BO additional 5 stitches at armhole edge. Work 1 row. Repeat from *; BO remaining 5 stitches.

*Front right*
Repeat front left, reversing shaping.

*Sleeves (make 2)*
With Denim, CO 30 (34, 36, 36, 38, 39, 41, 41). Work 2 rows stockinette stitch.
*Sleeve increase row (worked on RS)*: K1f&b, knit to last stitch, k1f&b.
Work *sleeve increase row* every RS row thirteen times. [56 (60, 62, 62, 64, 65, 67, 67) stitches]. Work even for 25 (23, 21, 19, 17, 15, 13, 11) rows, ending with a WS row. [52 (50, 48, 46, 44, 42, 40, 38) rows worked].
*Upper arm shaping*
Work *sleeve increase row*. Repeat *sleeve increase row* every fifth RS row 3 (3, 3, 3, 3, 3, 4, 4) times. Work even for 5 (7, 9, 13, 15, 17, 11, 13) rows. [88 (88, 88, 90, 90, 90, 92, 92) rows worked and 64 (68, 70, 70, 72, 73, 77, 77) stitches].
*Sleeve cap shaping*
BO 4 (4, 4, 4, 4, 3, 3, 3) stitches at the beginning of each of the next two rows. Then BO 2 (2, 2, 2, 3, 3, 3, 3) stitches at the beginning of each of the next two rows. [52 (56, 58, 56, 58, 61, 65, 65) stitches].
*Sleeve cap decrease row (worked on RS)*: K1, ssk, knit to last three stitches, k2tog, k1.
Repeat *sleeve cap decrease row* every RS row 13 (13, 14, 14, 15, 16, 16, 17) times. Work even 1 row, ending with a WS row.
BO 2 (2, 2, 2, 2, 2, 3, 3) stitches at the beginning of each of the next two rows. Then BO 3 (3, 3, 3, 3, 3, 3, 2) stitches at the beginning of each of the next two rows. BO remaining 14 (16, 16, 16, 16, 17, 19, 19) stitches.

## Finishing

Block pieces to measurements in blocking chart on page 148. Sew shoulder seams.

With Denim and smaller crochet hook, reinforce along neckline by working a slip stitch crochet along the inside of the front and back neckline 2 stitches in from the edge. Turn so right side of work is facing you and then slip stitch along the outside edge as well.

*Collar*
With larger crochet hook and Dove, make a chain to fit around the neckline, slightly stretched.
Row 1: Sc in second chain from hook, sc in each chain to end, ch 1. Turn.
Row 2: Sc in each sc, ch 1. Turn.
*Note*: Recheck your length against the neckline at this point. Depending on how tightly or loosely you chained, you may need to adjust. Better to rip back here than after you've finished the collar!
Row 3: (Sc, 4 dc) in first stitch, then dc in each sc to last sc, (4 dc, 1 sc) in last sc, ch 1. Turn.
Row 4: Sc in first stitch, dc in second stitch, then working in spaces between previous row of dc, work 2 dc in each space to last 2 stitches, 1 dc, 1 sc, ch 1. Turn.
Row 5: Sc in first stitch, dc in second stitch, then trc to last 2 stitches, dc, sc, ch 4. Turn.
Row 6: Sc in first stitch, ch 4, sc in second stitch, * ch 4, sk 1, sc in next stitch; repeat from * to last 2 stitches, ch 4, sc in next to last stitch, ch 4, sc in last stitch. Turn.
Row 7: Repeat row 6, but working the sc under the ch-4 loops.
Row 8: Repeat row 7.
Row 9: *Ch 3, sc under loop, ch 3, sc in sc; repeat from * to end. Turn.
Row 10: Work 3 sc under each loop only, skipping the sc of previous row.
Tie off.
Pin collar to neckline, easing any minor fullness. Using Dove and working from RS, backstitch collar to the jacket through the first row of sc, leaving the foundation chain overhanging the jacket slightly to fully cover the edge. Backstitch a second time one row in.

Set in sleeves, but do not stitch side seams.

*Cuffs*
Reinforce the curved sleeve edges using the same technique as used for the collar. Following instructions for collar, work cuffs for both sleeves, making the chain fit one knitted stitch short of the edge (to allow for seaming the sleeve). Stitch cuffs to sleeves, leaving sleeve selvedge stitches open.
Stitch side and sleeve seams. Weave in all ends.

*Front and bottom edging*
Using smaller crochet hook and Denim, starting at base of v-neck opening (below collar) and right side facing you, work as follows:
Row 1: Work a sc in 2 out of 3 rows of knitting (sc in first row, sc in second row, skip one row). At bottom corner, work 3 sc in corner. Across bottom, sc in 3 of 4 CO stitches. At corner, work 3 sc in corner stitch. Work back up the remaining front edge, working one sc in 2 out of 3 row stitches. Turn.
Row 2: *Ch 3, sk 2 sc, sc in third sc; repeat to end, skipping only one stitch for the three stitches at each corner. Turn.
Row 3: *Work 3 sc under ch loop, sc in sc of previous row; repeat from * to end.
Tie off.

Sew button to top of v-neck opening, using one of the chain edges as the button loop.

## Tips

- If you've never crocheted before, this a great first project. It's super speedy and may make a crocheter out of you. We have videos on PlanetPurl.com for all the basic crochet stitches.

- Pressed for time? You can replace the crochet work with purchased wide crochet-type lace available at fabric stores.

# Crazy Good Cornbread

*If you're not of the Southern persuasion, you might think, "Cornbread is cornbread." Not so, and this recipe is proof. Rich and slightly sweet, light and with just the right amount of crumb-iness, all it needs is to be slathered with butter while hot out of the oven. Of course, if you want to drizzle it with honey and call it breakfast, we won't tell.*

## Directions

Preheat oven to 425 degrees.

Butter and preheat a 9" cast iron skillet or a glass pie pan.

Stir together the dry ingredients. Beat together the buttermilk and melted butter. Beat the egg and add it to the buttermilk mixture. Add the corn to the buttermilk mixture. Add the wet ingredients all at once to the dry ingredients, stirring as little as possible. The batter should have some lumpiness to it. Pour into the preheated skillet or pie pan.

Bake until golden brown and toothpick inserted in center comes out clean, about 20 minutes. Serve piping hot. Cut into wedges, slather with real butter. If serving for breakfast, slather with butter and orange blossom honey.

## Shopping List

- 1 1/4 cups unbleached white flour
- 3/4 cup stone ground cornmeal
- 5 tsp baking powder
- 1 egg, room temperature
- 1 1/4 cups buttermilk
- 2/3 cup white sugar
- 3/4 tsp salt
- 2 Tbl melted butter
- 1/2 cup fresh corn, cooked and cut from the cob (approx. 1 cob), or frozen corn, thawed

Fast horses and smooth bourbon, Abe Lincoln and Daniel Boone, George Clooney and Johnny Depp— there are plenty of things to love about Kentucky!

Every May, the first two come together in the rose-covered pageantry of the Kentucky Derby, the first jewel of racing's Triple Crown. But you don't have to be an elite jockey to ride a champion horse over miles of rolling green hills. Dozens of riding schools provide vacation packages all throughout Bluegrass Country. Prefer a holiday with both boots on the ground? Several championship thoroughbred training centers are also open for tours.

Did you know that 95% of the world's bourbon is distilled in Kentucky? Follow the Kentucky Bourbon Trail to find 14 distilleries open to the public, all within about an hour of each other. Popular labels like Maker's Mark, Jim Beam, Woodford Reserve, Four Roses, Heaven Hill, and my favorite, Wild Turkey, are all available to be toured. See bourbon in its natural habitat, but bring a designated driver, since every tour includes a tasting. Back in Louisville, an "Urban Bourbon Trail" marks bars that serve at least 50 different kinds of bourbon. Of course no trip to Kentucky would be complete without at least one Mint Julep, served in a frosty silver cup.

Throughout Kentucky, time stands still in designated Heritage Towns where you can still experience the small-town life of days gone by. A favorite destination for textile artists is quaint Paducah, home of the National Quilt Museum. Another "can't-miss" is the Shaker Village of Pleasant Hill, the largest restored Shaker community in the country. Its 14 original and 20 restored Shaker buildings and over 3,000 acres of native prairies and fields are edged with miles of hand-laid rock walls. Costumed interpreters depict 18th century Shaker life, while craftsmen and women demonstrate their trades. And of course you can shop for beautiful Shaker furniture and craft items.

Kentucky is the perfect place to kick back, relax, and enjoy. If you want to do that while sipping a fine bourbon, well, "When in Kentucky...."

# Derby Day Clutch

## Churchill Downs, Kentucky

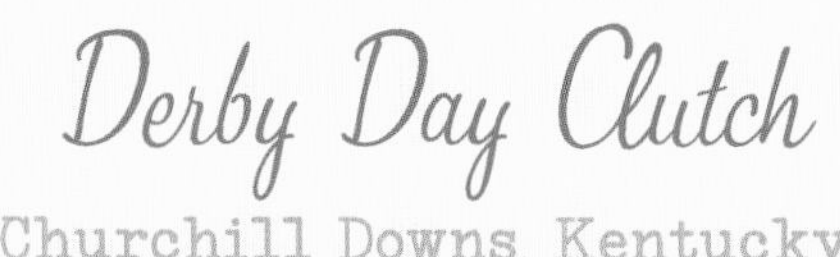

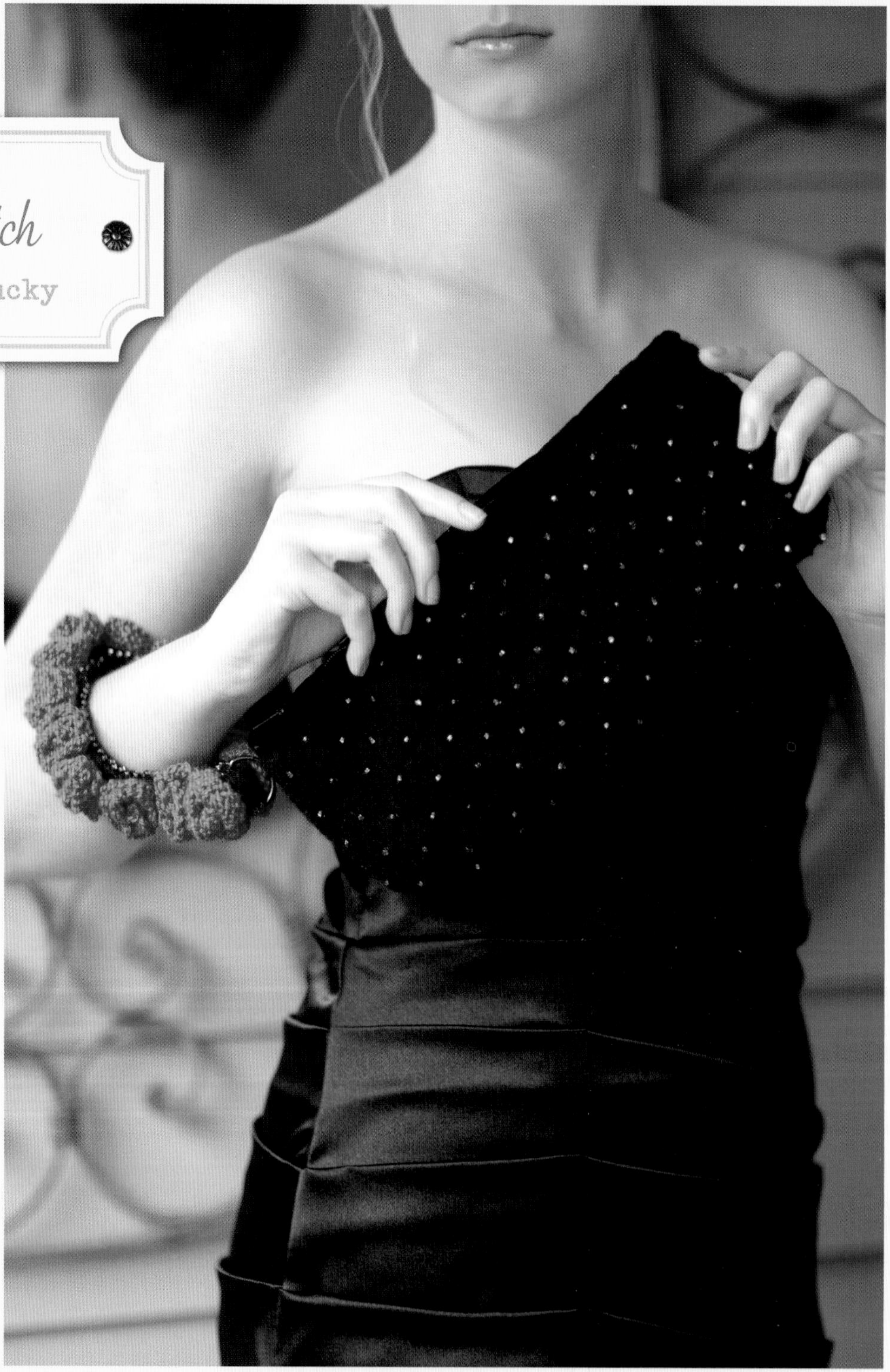

*Every spring Churchill Downs hosts horse racing's most famous event, the Kentucky Derby. For some, the event on the track is secondary to the chic competition in the grandstands as Louisville's ladies and the rest of polite society attempt to outdo each other with outlandish hats and the latest fashions.*

*The winner of the Derby gets in on the game with his or her own spectacular accessory— a gorgeous signature circlet of fresh red roses. But why should the horse have all the fun? This felted and beaded clutch has its own circlet of roses surrounding your wrist like a floral bracelet. Whip up this bag to celebrate your own winning style.*

## About this Project

**Skill Level:** Intermediate

**Finished Size:** Bag finished size 11" (28cm) wide by 4¾" (12cm) tall after felting; wrist strap finished size 1" (2.5cm) wide by 13" (33cm) circumference after felting

**Project Gauge:** 22 stitches and 32 rows = approximately 4" (10cm) in pattern on larger needle with one strand each of *220 Wool* and *Alpaca Lace* held together, after felting

## Stitch Guide

*Pb (place bead)*
Knit to stitch to be beaded. Bring yarn to front. Push bead up to right hand needle. Slip the stitch to be beaded purlwise with yarn in front. Bring yarn to back and knit the next stitch, pulling the beaded "collar" around the slipped stitch, making sure to keep bead to the front of the work, and snug it to the stitch.

*Beaded sc (beaded single crochet)*
Insert hook into stitch from front to back, yarn over hook and pull up loop. Push bead up to hook. Yarn over hook and pull through both loops, pulling bead into stitch.

## Instructions

*Bag*
Thread 100 beads onto *Alpaca Lace*. With larger needle and one strand each of *220 Wool* and *Alpaca Lace* held together, CO 120 stitches, placing marker after stitch 60. Join to work in the round, placing unique marker to mark beginning of round and being careful not to twist stitches.
Work chart *or* follow these written instructions:
Round 1: *Sl1 kwise wyib, knit to marker, slip marker; repeat from * to end.
Round 2: *K3, (pb, k5) nine times, pb, k2, slip marker; repeat from * to end.
Round 3: *Sl1 kwise wyib, knit to marker, slip marker; repeat from * to end.
Round 4: Knit.
Round 5: *Sl1 kwise wyib, knit to marker, slip marker; repeat from * to end.
Round 6: *K6, (pb, k5) nine times, slip marker; repeat from * to end.
Round 7: *Sl1 kwise wyib, knit to marker, slip marker; repeat from * to end.
Round 8: Knit.
Repeat rounds 1-8 four times. Break *Alpaca Lace* as needed to add more beads, then rejoin. BO all stitches purlwise.

Turn bag inside out and fold in half with the slipped stitches at each end. Pin. Using back stitch, stitch bottom seam, angling at both bottom corners to take in the corner two stitches wide and two stitches high. Felt to finished measurements.

### Shopping List

Cascade Yarns *220 Wool* (100% wool, 220 yards/200m); 1 skein Black #8555

Cascade Yarns *Alpaca Lace* (100% baby alpaca, 437 yards/400m); 1 skein Black #1406

Blue Sky Alpacas *Alpaca Silk* (50% alpaca, 50% silk, 146 yards/133m); 1 skein Ruby #123

Size US 9 (5.5mm) 16" (40cm) circular needle

Size US 5 (3.75mm) needles for flowers

350 glass 2/0 beads

Beading needle

12" (30cm) black zipper

¼ yard (.5m) lining fabric

¾ yard (68cm) ¾" (2cm) black velvet ribbon

¾" (2cm) black D-ring

Black embroidery floss

(16) ½" (1.25cm) rhinestone buttons

Sewing needle and thread to match roses and bag

Pliers

*Wrist strap*
With larger needle and one strand of *220 Wool*, CO 80 stitches. Place marker and join for working in the round, being careful not to twist stitches. Work four rounds stockinette stitch. BO all stitches kwise. String *Alpaca Lace* with 80 beads. Place 1 *Beaded sc* in each bind off stitch. String another 80 beads on the *Alpaca Lace* and repeat in each cast on stitch. Felt to finished measurements.

*Roses (make 16)*
With smaller needles and one strand of *Alpaca Silk*, CO 36 stitches.
Row 1: Knit.
Row 2: K3, twist left hand needle 360 degrees, creating a twist in the knitting, *k6, twist left hand needle 360 degrees, creating twist in the knitting; repeat from * to last 3 stitches, k3.
Row 3: Knit.
Row 4: K2tog across. (18 stitches)
Row 5: Knit.
Row 6: Knit.
Row 7: Pass all stitches over the first stitch, one at a time.
Cut yarn, leaving a 6" (15cm) tail. Pull tail through remaining stitch and tie off.
Curl knitting into a 1" (2.5cm) diameter rose shape. Using tail and tapestry needle, stitch through all layers near center and whipstitch across back seam. With matching thread and sewing needle, stitch one rhinestone button to the center of each rose.

## Finishing

Fold ribbon in half, wrong sides together. Whipstitch velvet ribbon to inside edge of bag. Stitch in zipper, cutting zipper at bottom as needed and whipstitching across bottom of zipper tracks to prevent zipper from coming apart when unzipped. Cut piece of lining fabric to width of bag plus 1" (2.5cm) and twice the height of the bag, plus 1" (2.5cm). Fold in half with right sides together and stitch 1/2" (1cm) seams on both sides.

Slip lining into bag. Fold upper edges of lining to the wrong side and pin in place. Whipstitch lining to the bag. Fold ribbon to outside edge and whipstitch in place.

Using thread and sewing needle, stitch roses to the wrist strap, keeping them close together and evenly distributed along strap. Fold the strap in half between two roses and whipstitch in one spot at each edge about 1" (2.5cm) from end to create a tunnel for the D-ring. Open D-ring and slip it into the pocket created by the whipstitching. Using pliers, pinch D-ring closed. Using six strands of black embroidery floss, stitch the rounded end of the D-ring securely to the end of the bag closest to the zipper pull when the zipper is closed.

*Beading Chart*

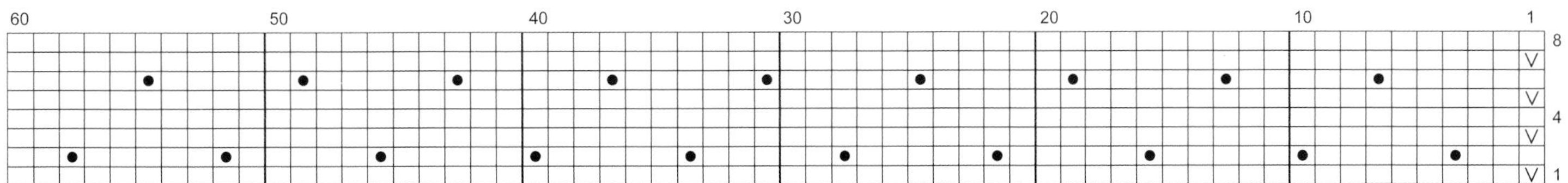


## Tips

- You may be tempted to put all the beads on the yarn at once, but restrain yourself. The yarn is slightly damaged by pushing the beads along and if you put too many beads on, it may break the yarn.
- Before felting the bag, check to make sure all beads are sitting on the outside. If any have wiggled to the inside, use a short strand of the *Alpaca Lace* and a sewing needle to stitch the bead in place on the front.
- If you're not comfortable with the single crochet beaded edging for the wrist strap, you can whipstitch the beads along the edge before felting, or just leave the strap plain.
- This bag is lovely for a wedding party, with the bag knitted to match the dresses and roses to match the bouquet.
- Pressed for time? Replace the knitted flowers with fabric flowers found in the bridal section of fabric stores.
- General felting instructions are provided in the Mardi Gras Party Bangles pattern.
- You can find a free beaded knitting class on PlanetPurl.com.

*The tradition of roses at the Kentucky Derby started in 1896, when the winner, Ben Brush, received pink roses. Red roses became the official flower of the Derby in 1904.*

# Summer Breeze Socks

Louisville, Kentucky

*Summertime in Kentucky is best enjoyed in the evenings, after the sun sets. Dusk banishes the blistering heat and humidity, replacing it with warm breezes, the soft perfume of night-blooming flowers, and the nearly magical appearance of fireflies. These lovely socks designed by* ***Elise Williams*** *of* ***Sophie's Fine Yarn Shoppe*** *celebrate soft summer nights with their breeze-loving flower petal lace design and golden firefly color.*

## About this Project

**Skill Level:** Intermediate

**Finished Size:** To fit average woman, approximately 8" (20cm) circumference

**Project Gauge:** 38 stitches = 4" (10cm) in *Summer Breeze Stitch*

## Shopping List

Lorna's Laces *Shepherd Sock* (80% superwash wool, 20% nylon, 435 yards/398m); 1 skein Firefly

US 1.5 (2.5mm) double pointed needles (set of 5)

Stitch marker

Tapestry needle

## Stitch Guide

*Twisted Rib (on even number of stitches)*
All rounds: *K1tbl, p1; repeat from * to end.

*Summer Breeze Stitch (worked over multiples of 13; sock begins with 78 stitches)*
Round 1: *Ssk, k9, k2tog; repeat from * to end. (66 stitches)
Round 2: Knit.
Round 3: *Ssk, k7, k2tog; repeat from * to end. (54 stitches)
Round 4: Knit.
Round 5: *Ssk, yo, [k1, yo] 5 times, k2tog; repeat from * to end. (78 stitches)
Round 6: Purl.
Repeat rounds 1-6 until desired length.

## Instructions

*Cuff*
CO 72 stitches using long-tail method. Place marker and join for working in the round, being careful not to twist stitches. Work *Twisted Rib* for 12 rounds.
*Begin Summer Breeze pattern*
Set up round: *K12, m1; repeat from * to end. (78 stitches)
Work 12 repeats of *Summer Breeze* pattern, ending with round 6.
*Heel*
Row 1: Knit 19 stitches from needle 1 onto needle 4, turn.
Row 2: Sl1 pwise wyif, p36, p2tog.
You now have 38 heel stitches on one needle. Distribute the remaining 39 stitches evenly over two other needles.
Row 3: *Sl1, k1; repeat from * across the 38 heel stitches. Turn.
Row 4: Sl1, p 38. Turn.
Repeat rows 3-4 until a total of 38 heel rows have been worked.
*Turn heel*
Row 1: Sl1, k20, ssk, k1, turn.
Row 2: Sl1, p5, p2tog, p1, turn.

Row 3: Sl1, k to one stitch before gap, ssk (last stitch before and after gap), k1, turn.
Row 4: Sl1, p to one stitch before gap, p2tog (last stitch before and after gap), p1, turn.
Repeat rows 3-4 until you have worked all stitches, ending with a wrong side (purl) row. You should have 22 heel stitches remaining.

*Gusset*

Round 1: Sl1, k10. The round now begins here. With new needle (this will be needle 1) knit 11 remaining heel stitches, pick up and knit 19 stitches along first side of heel flap, work in *Summer Breeze* pattern across needles 2 and 3, then using empty needle (needle 4) pick up and knit 19 stitches along other side of heel flap, and knit 11 stitches from heel turn onto this needle.

*Note*: You will now have 99 stitches on the needles— 30 each on needles 1 and 4, and 39 divided over needles 2 and 3.

Round 2: Needle 1 – knit to 3 stitches from end of needle, k2tog, k1; needles 2 and 3 - work in *Summer Breeze* pattern; needle 4 - k1, ssk, knit to end of needle.
Round 3: Needle 1 – knit; needles 2 and 3 – work in *Summer Breeze* pattern; needle 4 – knit.
Repeat rounds 2-3 until 19 stitches remain on needles 1 and 4. (77 stitches total).

*Foot*

Continue working as established (knitting stitches on needles 1 and 4, and working *Summer Breeze* pattern on needles 2 and 3) until sock is 2" (5cm) shorter than desired length, ending with round 5 of *Summer Breeze* pattern.

*Toe*

Set up: Needle 1 – knit; needle 2, purl; needle 3 – purl to last two stitches, p2tog; needle 4 – knit. (76 stitches). Knit across needle 1 – the round now begins with needle 2.
Round 1: Needle 2 – k1, ssk, knit to end; needle 3 – knit until 3 stitches remain, k2tog, k1; needle 4 – k1, ssk, knit to end; needle 1 – knit until 3 stitches remain, k2tog, k1.
(4 stitches decreased).
Round 2: Knit.
Repeat rounds 1-2 until 36 stitches remain; then repeat round 1 only until 16 stitches remain.
Cut yarn leaving 8" (20cm) tail. Close the toe using Kitchener stitch. Weave in all ends.

Shop owner *Barbara Franc* learned to knit from her mother, Sophie. Barbara and designer *Elise Williams* invite you to bring your knitting and join them on the sofa when you're visiting Louisville. SophiesFineYarn.com.

*Summer Breeze Stitch Chart*

| 13 | 12 | 11 | 10 | 9 | 8 | 7 | 6 | 5 | 4 | 3 | 2 | 1 | |
|---|---|---|---|---|---|---|---|---|---|---|---|---|---|
| ● | ● | ● | ● | ● | ● | ● | ● | ● | ● | ● | ● | ● | 6 |
| / | O | | O | | O | | O | | O | | O | \ | 5 |
| | | | | | | | | | | | | | 4 |
| / | ■ | ■ | | | | | | | | ■ | ■ | \ | 3 |
| | | | | | | | | | | | | | 2 |
| / | ■ | | | | | | | | | | ■ | \ | 1 |

\ ssk

■ placeholder - no stitch

□ knit

/ k2tog

O yarnover

● purl

# Mint Julep

*There's a good reason this is the official drink of the Kentucky Derby. Just the name brings to mind white linen suits, expansive porches, and horse-drawn carriages on long tree-lined driveways. The crushed mint, sweet syrup, smooth bourbon and traditional frosty silver cup combine to make a beverage fit for the fashion parade at Churchill Downs.*

## Directions

Make a simple syrup by boiling sugar and water together for five minutes. Cool and place in a covered container with six or eight sprigs of fresh mint, then refrigerate overnight.

Make one drink at a time by filling a julep cup with crushed ice. Add 2 ounces of whiskey and 1 tablespoon of the mint syrup. Stir to frost the outside of the cup. Garnish with a sprig of fresh mint and serve with a straw.

### Shopping List

- 2 cups sugar
- 2 cups water
- Sprigs of fresh mint
- Crushed ice
- Kentucky whiskey
- Silver julep serving cups

American history comes alive in Virginia. With 120 National Historic Landmarks and 13 National Historic Parks, you can't swing a tri-corner hat without hitting a national treasure. Virginia's citizens played a leading role in the founding of the country. George Washington and Thomas Jefferson were just two of the Revolutionary War patriots who were born here. One hundred years later, Virginia would serve as capital of the Confederacy. So whether it's Revolutionary or Civil War history you seek, Virginia has it all.

If it's your first visit to Virginia, head to the historic triangle of Jamestown, Yorktown and Williamsburg. Jamestown Settlement includes a re-creation of the 1607 colonists' fort and a Powhatan village. Yorktown Victory Center marks the site of the British surrender to General George Washington on October 19, 1781. In addition to the indoor exhibits, there is an outdoor living history museum with a re-created Continental Army encampment and a 1780s farm, both with costumed interpreters providing glimpses of life during the Revolutionary War.

My favorite spot for a holiday trip is Colonial Williamsburg. Preserved and restored in large part through the generosity of John D. Rockefeller, Jr., the 300+ acre site contains hundreds of buildings with costumed interpreters portraying colonial life. A meal at one of the restored tavern restaurants is a must, and in the evenings you can catch a candlelit concert at the Governor's Palace.

If I could move anywhere in the South, it would have to be the Shenandoah Valley, in Virginia's northwestern corner. 18th and 19th century towns with real Main Streets, town squares and band gazebos, with the beloved Blue Ridge Mountains as their backdrop is my idea of paradise. For the best views, Skyline Drive twists and turns for 105 miles through Shenandoah National Park. The road is dotted with historic lodges where you can get a meal with a view, stay for extraordinary hiking or even stop at a trailhead for a short hike to a gorgeous waterfall. Barely an hour from Washington D.C., Shenandoah National Park is the unspoiled America explored by the first settlers who came to this country.

# Honeysuckle Bridal Set

Gloucester, Virginia

*When mid-summer rolls around down South, most flowering plants take a vacation and return with the cooler temperatures. Where lesser flowers fail, honeysuckle thrives, gracing trellises and encircling mailbox posts through the dog days of summer.*

*This bridal set was inspired by golden, sweetly-perfumed John Clayton honeysuckle twining in latticework. This lovely flower is a true Virginia native, having been first identified during colonial times in the churchyard of Gloucester's historic 17th century Abingdon Episcopal Church.*

*The sparkling aurora borealis crystals that adorn the bag and gloves evoke the perfect droplets of sweet nectar that give honeysuckle its name. The blooms can be knit in any color— blossoms of blue delphinium, lilac asters, pink campanulas, or white jasmine, for a start. In any color, the set adds a feminine floral touch to a lucky bride's wedding day.*

## About this Project

**Skill Level:** Intermediate

**Finished Sizes:** Bag: 20" (50cm) in circumference by 10" (25cm) high

Gloves: Approximately 6½" (16.5cm) circumference unstretched

Garter: S/M and L/XL; 1¾" (4.5cm) high and 25 (30)" [63 (76)cm] in circumference before adding elastic

**Project Gauge:** 3 repeats wide and 12 rows (1 repeat) of *Lattice Lace* on larger needles = 5" (13cm) wide and 2" (5cm) high after blocking

## Stitch Guide

*Beaded sc (for bag and glove edging)*
Put hook through the top loop only of the knit bind off. Yarn over and pull up a loop. Push a bead up to the hook. Yarn over and pull through both loops, capturing the bead in the stitch.

*Lattice Lace (worked over repeats of 8 plus 5)*
*Note:* Stitch count varies. Count only after rows 5, 6, 11, and 12.
Row 1(RS): K2, *k2tog, k1, yo, k1, ssk, k2; repeat from * to last 3 stitches, k3.
Row 2 and all WS rows: Purl.
Row 3: K1,*k2tog, k1, [yo, k1] twice, ssk; repeat from * to last 4 stitches, k4.
Row 5: K3, *yo, k3, yo, k1, ssk, k1; repeat from * to last 2 stitches, k2.
Row 7: K5, *k2tog, k1, yo, k1, ssk, k2; repeat from * to end.
Row 9: K4, *k2tog, k1, [yo, k1] twice, ssk; repeat from * to last stitch, k1.
Row 11: K3, *k2tog, k1, yo, k3, yo, k1; repeat from * to last 2 stitches, k2.
Row 12: Purl.
Repeat rows 1-12.

*Lattice Lace Chart*

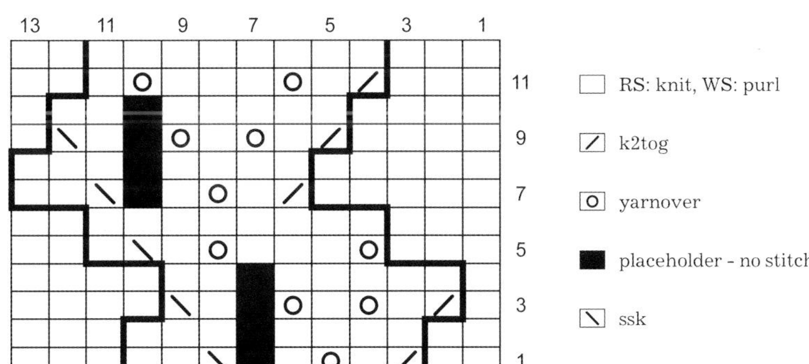

## Shopping List

Dark Horse Yarns *Desert Flower* (100% mercerized cotton, 125 yards/114m); 2 skeins White #DF801, 1 skein each Yellow #DF820 and Green #DF850

Size 8 cotton DMC *Perle* mercerized crochet cotton; 1 small ball White

Size US 6 (4mm) needles

Size US 6 (4mm) 16" (40cm) circular needle

Size US 4 (3.5mm) double pointed needles

Small crochet hook

206 4mm bicone aurora borealis crystal beads for gloves and bag

Tapestry needle

½ yard (.5m) crepe-back satin in soft yellow, or other double-sided, silky lining fabric and matching sewing thread

Safety pin

12-18" (30-46cm) of ½" (1.25cm) wide knit elastic

Small amount ⅜" (1cm) wide pale green ribbon

½" (1.25cm) crystal button (shown with JHB #766)

Fray Check (optional)

## Instructions

### Bag

With larger needles and White, CO 101 stitches.
Row 1 (RS): Knit.
Row 2 (WS): Purl.
*Begin Lattice Lace pattern*
*For Bag, stitch counts of each row of 12 row pattern are as follows: rows 1-4= 89; rows 5-6= 101; rows 7-10= 89; rows 11-12= 101*
Row 3-50: Work *Lattice Lace* pattern for 4 repeats (48 rows).
Row 51: Knit.
Row 52: Purl.
Row 53-54: Repeat rows 51-52.
Row 55: Knit.
Row 56: Purl, decreasing 3 stitches evenly across the row. (98 stitches)
*Eyelet row*
Row 57: K3, *BO 2 stitches, k4; repeat from * to last 5 stitches, BO 2 stitches, k3.
Row 58: Purl, casting on 2 stitches over each BO using backward loop cast on.
Row 59: Knit.
Row 60: Purl.
Row 61-62: Repeat rows 59-60.
*Top ruffle*
Row 63: K1f&b across. (196 stitches)
Row 64: Purl.
Row 65: Knit.
Row 66: Purl.
BO very loosely. Block to 20" (51cm) x 8" (20cm), not including ruffle at top edge. Do not block ruffle. Allow ruffle to curl while drying. Stitch side seam, taking in full selvedge stitches.
*Bag bottom*
With larger circular needle and White, pick up and knit 99 stitches along bottom edge of bag. Place marker and join for working in the round.
Rounds 1 and 2: Knit.
Round 3: *K7, k2tog; repeat from * to end. (88 stitches)
Round 4 and all even rounds: Knit.
Round 5: *K6, k2tog; repeat from * to end. (77 stitches)
Round 7: *K5, k2tog; repeat from * to end. (66 stitches)
Round 9: *K4, k2tog; repeat from * to end. (55 stitches)
Round 11: *K3, k2tog; repeat from * to end. (44 stitches)
Round 13: *K2, k2tog; repeat from * to end. (33 stitches)
Round 15: *K1, k2tog; repeat from * to end. (22 stitches)
Round 17: K2tog eleven times. (11 stitches)
Round 19: K2tog five times, k1. (6 stitches)
Draw yarn through remaining stitches and secure on inside.

*Vine drawstrings (make 2, one of each length)*
With smaller double pointed needles and Green, CO 7 stitches, leaving a 6" (15cm) tail.
*Decreasing bud base (worked back and forth)*
Row 1 (RS): Knit.
Row 2 and all WS rows: Purl.
Row 3: K2, k2tog, knit to end. (6 stitches)
Row 5: K2, k2tog, knit to end. (5 stitches)
Row 7: K2, k2tog, knit to end. (4 stitches)
Row 9: K1, k2tog, k1. Do not turn. (3 stitches)

With right side facing begin working three stitch I-cord. Work I-cord until piece measures 38" (97cm) from CO edge.

*Increasing bud base (worked back and forth)*
Row 1 (RS): Knit.
Row 2 and all WS rows: Purl.
Row 3: K1, k1f&b, k1. (4 stitches)
Row 5: K2, k1f&b, k1. (5 stitches)
Row 7: K2, k1f&b, k2. (6 stitches)
Row 9: K2, k1f&b, k3. (7 stitches)
Row 10: Purl.
BO all stitches, leaving 6" (15cm) tail.
Make a second drawstring, working I-cord until the piece measures 42" (107cm) from CO edge and finishing with an *increasing bud base* as above.

Weave one drawstring through the bag starting at the seam of the bag with the center of the drawstring on the outside of the bag and going into the first eyelet on each side of the seam, weaving in and out of the next 5 eyelets. For second drawstring, start with center of drawstring on the outside of the bag at the space where the ends of the first drawstring exit the bag. Weave into the first eyelet on each side and continue weaving in and out of the remaining 5 eyelets. The first drawstring exits the bag where the second drawstring enters the bag; the second drawstring exits the bag where the first drawstring enters the bag. Pull bag open. Arrange the drawstrings so that the bud base ends are staggered, rather than equal on either side. *(See photo for guide).* Knot the pairs of the ends of each drawstring near the bag.

*Vine branches (make 8)*
Following the instructions for the vine drawstrings, knit 4 shorter vines, beginning with CO of 7 stitches, working the *decreasing bud base*, and knitting 4 cords to a length of 5" (13cm) from CO edge and 4 cords to a length of 7" (18cm) from CO edge. Finish each as follows:
Round 1: Continuing to work as in I-cord, k1, k2tog. (2 stitches)
Round 2: Continuing to work as in I-cord, k2.
Round 3: K2tog. (1 stitch)
Round 4: Knit.
Cut yarn, leaving 6" (15cm) tail. Pull tail through remaining stitch.

*Small honeysuckle blossoms (make 4)*
With smaller double pointed needles and Yellow, using knitted cast on, CO 10 stitches. BO 9 stitches. Do not cut yarn. *Slide remaining stitch to opposite end of needle, without turning. Using knitted cast on, CO 9 stitches. BO 9 stitches. Repeat from * until 5 petals have been cast on and bound off. After 5th petal, BO all stitches, leaving a 6-8" (15-20cm) tail. Repeat for required number of blossoms.

*Medium honeysuckle blossoms (make 4)*
With smaller double pointed needles and Yellow, using knitted cast on, CO 12 stitches. BO 11 stitches. Do not cut yarn. *Slide remaining stitch to opposite end of needle, without turning. Using knitted cast on, CO 11 stitches. BO 11 stitches. Repeat from * until 5 petals have been cast on and bound off. After 5th petal, BO all stitches, leaving a 6-8" (15-20cm) tail. Repeat for required number of blossoms.

*Large honeysuckle blossoms (make 4)*
With smaller double pointed needles and Yellow, using knitted cast on, CO 14 stitches. BO 13 stitches. Do not cut yarn. *Slide remaining stitch to opposite end of needle, without turning. Using knitted cast on, CO 13 stitches. BO 13 stitches. Repeat from * until 5 petals have been cast on and bound off. After 5th petal, BO all stitches, leaving a 6-8" (15-20cm) tail. Repeat for required number of blossoms.

**Garter**

With larger needles and White, CO 125 (149) stitches.
Row 1-2: Knit.
*Begin Lattice Lace pattern*
*For Garter, stitch counts of each row of 6 row pattern are as follows: rows 1-4= 110 (131); rows 5-6= 125 (149)*
Row 3-8: Work rows 1-6 of *Lattice Lace* pattern.
Cut yarn. Join Yellow.
Row 9 (RS): Knit.
Row 10 (WS): Purl.
Row 11: Knit.
Row 12: Purl.
*Turning ridge*
Row 13-14: Purl.
Row 15: Knit.
Row 16: Purl.
BO in purl.

### Gloves (make 2)

With larger needles and White, CO 37 stitches.
*Fingertip ribbing*
Row 1 (RS): K1, *p1, k1; repeat from * to end.
Row 2 (WS): P1,*k1, p1; repeat from * to end.
Row 3-4: Repeat rows 1-2.
*Begin Lattice Lace pattern*
*For Gloves, stitch counts of each row of 12 row pattern are as follows: rows 1-4= 33; rows 5-6= 37; rows 7-10= 33; rows 11-12= 37*
Row 5-28: Work two repeats of *Lattice Lace* pattern.
Row 29-33: Work rows 1-5 of *Lattice Lace* pattern.
Row 34: Purl, decreasing 10 stitches (p2tog) evenly across work. (27 stitches)
*Wrist ribbing and ruffle*
Row 35-42: Work 8 rows as for fingertip ribbing.
Row 43: Knit.
Row 44: Purl.
Row 45: K1f&b in each stitch. (54 stitches)
Row 46: Purl.
Row 47: Same as row 45. (108 stitches)
BO very loosely in knit.

## Finishing

*Bag*
*Beaded edge*
String 98 beads onto DMC *Perle* crochet cotton. Join crochet cotton at bag seam. Using small crochet hook, and putting hook through the loop of the bind off closest to the top edge only, work a *Beaded sc* in first stitch, slip stitch crochet in second stitch. Continue alternating *Beaded sc* and slip stitches until all bind off stitches have been worked and 98 beads have been placed.

*Lining*
Fold fabric in half. Lay bag on top. Using bag as a pattern, draw around bag, adding 1" (2.5cm) on sides and bottom for a double seam allowance and stopping 3/4" (2cm) above the beginning of the eyelet row. With crepe sides together and satin sides facing out, stitch side and bottom of bag with 3/8" (1cm) seams. Turn bag inside out so satin sides are together and crepe sides are facing out. Press flat. Seam again with 5/8" (1.5cm) seam to create a "French seam" that encases the loose fabric from the previous seam. Turn bag so satin sides are facing out. Press 1/2" (1cm) of top edge to outside of bag. Repeat, pressing another 1/2" (1cm) to outside of bag. Hem top of bag. Slip fabric bag into lace bag, pinning top edge 2 rows below eyelet row. Whipstitch in place using doubled thread.
*Blossoms and vines*
Block open bud base ends of vines. Block blossoms, pinning petals out flat to a length of 1 1/2" (3.75cm). Thread bind off tail of blossom through tapestry needle. Roll flower into a tight tube. Using threaded tail, stitch through the base of the flower. Weave in end at the base of flower and trim. Place the flower inside flat end of a vine. Using cast on tail of the vine, stitch through the blossom to hold in place. Use the remaining part of the cast on tail to whipstitch the bud base closed around the blossom. Knot at end and weave in end by running it through center of I-cord for 2-3" (5-8cm). Using photo as a guide, stitch 2 vine branches to each of the 4 drawstring ends. Weave in ends where branches join the vines by knotting the

yarn at base of branch, running remaining tail into center of I-cord tube for 2-3" (5-8cm) and trimming the remaining tail.

*Garter*
Block to 25 (30)" x 1 3/4" [63 (76)cm x 4.5cm], pinning to exaggerate scallop at bottom edge. When completely dry, stitch side seam. Weave in ends. Fold yellow top band to inside along purl ridge and pin in place. With Yellow, whipstitch bind off edge of casing to garter, leaving a 1" (2.5cm) opening. To determine length of elastic, measure around thigh of recipient, and subtract 10% (see *Tips* below). Cut elastic. Put a safety pin in one end of elastic and use pin to push elastic through casing, being careful not to twist elastic. Stitch ends of elastic together. Tuck elastic into casing and stitch remaining opening closed. With green ribbon, loop a small bow shape. Stitch bow to center front of garter (the seam is the center back), tacking through the knot of the bow to keep it from coming untied. Stitch a decorative crystal button to center of bow. Trim ends of ribbon. Apply fray stopping liquid to ends of bow if desired.

*Gloves*
Block lace section only to 6 3/4" (16.5cm) wide x 4 3/4" (12cm) high, not including ribbing or ruffle. Do not block ruffle or ribbing. Allow ruffle to curl while drying. Mattress stitch seam from bottom edge of ruffle to 1" (2.5cm) above wrist ribbing, and from top ribbed band down 2" (5cm), leaving remaining middle 2" (5cm) section open for thumb opening.

*Beaded edge*
String 54 beads onto DMC *Perle* crochet cotton. Turn one glove so that right side is facing you, with the stitched seam at right hand edge. Join crochet cotton at seam. Using small crochet hook, and putting hook through the loop of the bind off closest to the top edge only, work a *Beaded sc* in first stitch, slip stitch crochet in second stitch. Continue alternating *Beaded sc* and slip stitches until all bind off stitches have been worked and 54 beads placed. Repeat for second glove. Weave in ends.

*Southern Honeysuckle*
Although Southern honeysuckle varieties come in many colors, the sunny yellow and white variety is my favorite. I've grown honeysuckle on trellises in my own gardens over the years.

- Place a lifeline every 6-12 rows to give you a place to rip back if the unthinkable happens.
- This lace pattern is very stretchy and the gloves will fit most hands.
- The lace count changes in this pattern. The full stitch count (same as number of cast on stitches) is only on rows 5, 6, 11 and 12, so I have provided the stitch counts for each piece of the set to help you keep track.
- You can make these gloves sit a little higher on the wrist by adding extra rows of the wrist ribbing.
- A loose bind off on the ruffles is critical. If you tend to bind off tightly, bind off with a size 7 or 8 needle.
- Need a little "something blue" for the bride? String a single blue crystal bead on with the clear beads when applying the beaded edge to either the glove or bag.
- The beaded crochet edge is super simple, but you can also stitch the beads on with the crochet cotton. Take one whipstitch in each bind off stitch, placing a crystal bead for every other stitch.
- If you don't know the recipient's leg size, use these estimates for elastic length: 12" (S), 14" (M), 16" (L) and 18" (XL). (30, 36, 41, 46cm).
- Don't add beads to the garter. They can damage delicate dress fabrics.
- The gloves make a lovely accessory for the bridesmaids, knit in colors to match their gowns.
- For a pretty decoration for an updo hairstyle, knit a few double-ended vines and a mix of blossom sizes. Assemble and then tie a half-hitch knot off-center of the vine. Push hairpins through the back of the knot and arrange in your hair.

# Blue Ridge Lap Throw

## Shenandoah Valley, Virginia

*In the mostly flat South, the Blue Ridge Mountains are our "purple mountains majesty," except for the fact they're more blue and gray than purple. But you know what I mean. The Blue Ridge range runs from Georgia, through the Carolinas, Tennessee, Virginia and West Virginia, then into Pennsylvania.*

*This scrumptiously soft lap throw is inspired by those same gorgeous peaks. Two simple decreases create the mountain-shaped wedges. The ombré border evokes the dusky colors of the mountains, and the subtle tone-on-tone designs created in simple reverse stockinette celebrate the flora, fauna and historic cabins of the Blue Ridge's Shenandoah National Park. This throw is a perfect accompaniment to a snuggling session, even if you're in Florida with the air conditioning turned up and are just dreaming of the mountains. Unfortunately, the romantic fireplace, hot chocolate and a sexy someone to share it with are not included with the pattern.*

## About this Project

**Skill Level:** Easy-mediate

**Finished Size:** Approximately 58" (145cm) in diameter

**Project Gauge:** 12 stitches and 16 rows = 4" (10cm) in stockinette stitch with two strands of yarn held together.

*Note:* Gauge is not critical but will impact the finished size and the amount of yarn used.

### Shopping List

Valley Yarns *Stockbridge* (50% alpaca, 50% wool, 109 yards/100m); 13 skeins Natural, 7 skeins Deep Teal, 5 skeins Colonial Blue

Size US 13 (9mm) 36" (90cm) circular needle

Stitch markers

Tapestry needle

## Instructions

*Note:* The circular needle is used to accommodate the large number of stitches. Work back and forth and do not join as for circular knitting.

With two strands of Deep Teal held together, CO 542 stitches, placing markers after stitches 91, 181, 271, 361, and 451. You will have 91 stitches in the first and last groups of stitches and 90 in each of the middle 4 sections. The first and last stitches of every row are edge stitches used to seam the throw together. Knit the first and last stitch of every right side row and purl the first and last stitch of every wrong side row to create a stockinette stitch edge for easier seaming.
Row 1 (RS): Knit.
Row 2 (WS): P1, knit to last stitch, p1.
Row 3: K1, *ssk (left leaning decrease), knit to two stitches before marker, k2tog (right leaning decrease), slip marker; repeat from * to last stitch, k1. (530 stitches)
Row 4: P1, knit to last stitch, slipping markers as they present, p1.
Row 5-10: Repeat rows 3-4 three times more. (494 stitches: 83 in each end section, 82 in each middle section)
Break off one strand of Deep Teal and join one strand of Colonial Blue. You will work the next 10 rows with one strand each of Deep Teal and Colonial Blue.
Row 11-20: Repeat rows 3-4 five times. (434 stitches: 73 in each end section, 72 in each middle section)
Break off strand of Deep Teal and join second strand of Colonial Blue. You will work the next 10 rows with two strands of Colonial Blue.
Row 21-30: Repeat rows 3-4 five times. (374 stitches: 63 in each end section, 62 in each middle section)
Break off both strands of Colonial Blue and join two strands of Natural. The remainder of the project is worked with two strands of Natural held together.
*Note:* Rows 31 and 32 are set up rows for the charted patterns. Row 31 is an increase row.
Row 31: K1, *ssk, (k4, k1f&b, k5, k1f&b) five times, knit to last 2 stitches before marker, k2tog, slip marker; repeat from * in each of the remaining five sections; k1 on last stitch of row. (422 stitches: 70 in each middle section resulting from ten increases and the two decreases in each section, and 71 in each end section)
Row 32: Purl.
Begin charted pattern. *Note:* Row 33 of project is the first row of the chart. Odd numbered (RS) rows of chart are worked right to left and even numbered (WS) rows of

The Blue Ridge Mountains' palette of ombréd blues inspired the edge treatment of this lap throw. The tone-on-tone designs celebrate the wildlife and forests found in the Shenandoah National Park.

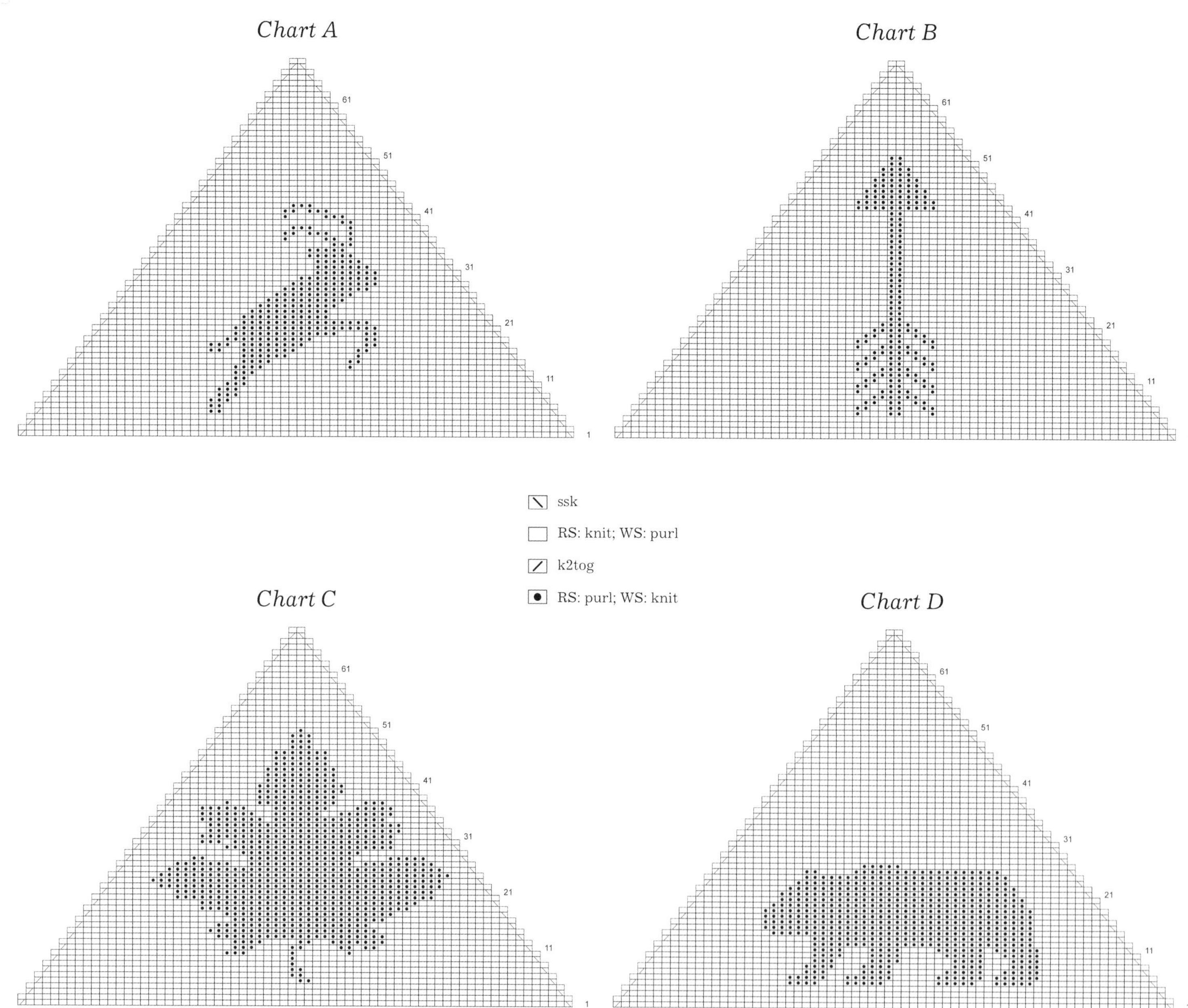

Chart A
61
51
41
31
21
11
1
Chart B
61
51
41
31
21
11
1
ssk
RS: knit; WS: purl
k2tog
RS: purl; WS: knit
Chart C
61
51
41
31
21
11
1
Chart D
61
51
41
31
21
11
1

## Chart E

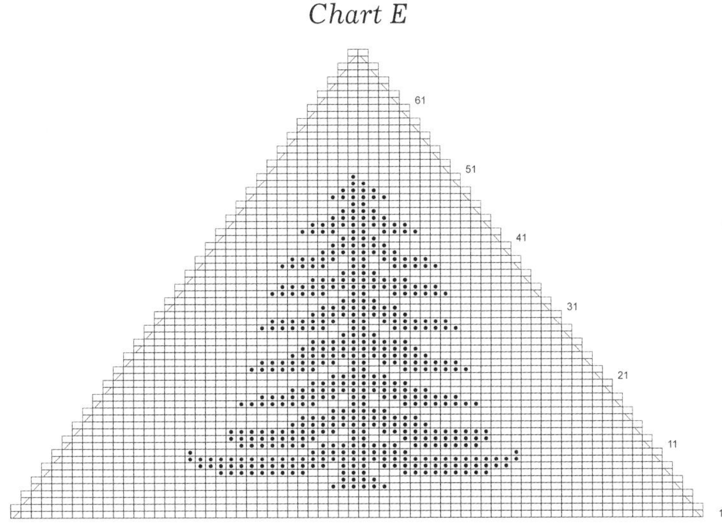


## Chart F

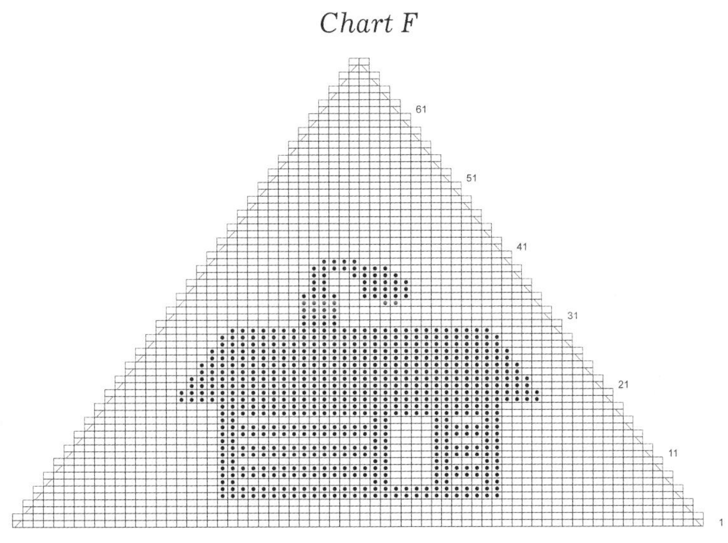

chart are worked from left to right. The seam edge stitches (first stitch on panel A and last stitch on the last panel F) are not included on charts A and F.
Row 33-100:
Odd numbered rows (RS): K1, begin corresponding row of chart A, then B, C, D, E and F; k1.
Even numbered rows (WS): P1, begin corresponding row of chart F, then E, D, C, B and A; p1.
At completion of charts, a total of 14 stitches remain.
Row 101: BO 1 kwise, k2tog six times, removing markers, k1. (7 stitches)
Row 102: BO 1 pwise, purl to end. (6 stitches)
Cut yarn leaving 6" (15cm) tail. Draw yarn through remaining stitches and tie off.

## Finishing

Using one strand of Deep Teal and mattress stitch, sew up seam of outside twenty rows of border section, capturing both stockinette edge stitches in seam. Repeat for inner ten rows of border with one strand of Colonial Blue. With one strand of Natural and mattress stitch, sew up seam of main section, including both edge stitches in seam. Weave in ends. Lightly block by spraying one section at a time with warm water and pinning out the reverse stockinette stitch design to highlight it. Allow to dry.

## Tips

- If the idea of casting on 542 stitches makes your head spin, you can knit this blanket in individual wedges. Cast on 92 stitches for each section so that you have a single extra stitch on each edge for seaming. Work these seam stitches with a knit on the right side and a purl on the wrong side. These stitches are not included in the charts.

- For edge stitches, resist the urge to create a slip stitch edge instead of stockinette. Since the blanket is knit at a looser gauge than suggested for the yarn, you'll want extra stability in the seam.

- I recommend sewing up the throw using mattress stitch and working from the right side, making it easier to keep your increase and decrease ridge nice and neat. The increases and decreases, when sewn together side by side, create a decorative ridge that is part of the design.

- I chose teal and dark blue for the contrast border as they remind me of the colors of the mountains at dusk. The border can be knitted in a solid color if you choose, or if you want the graduated color, it would look equally nice in a brown and dark tan combination, or dark and medium olive. Just choose two shades in the same color family that harmonize and where the color shift isn't too jarring. The tone-on-tone detail will show best in a light color.

- If you substitute yarns, choose something in a light worsted weight— 20 stitches = 4" (10cm) on US 7 (4.5mm) needles— to duplicate the soft drape.

# Chocolate Toffee Pecan Pie

*Pecan pie is a staple on menus all through the South. How do you improve on a dessert made with crunchy sweet pecans resting on a layer of sticky sugary filling? Add mini chocolate chips and crushed toffee. The toffee melts into the filling and adds an incredible buttery yumminess while the chocolate adds ... well, it's chocolate. Need we say more?*

## Directions

Preheat oven to 350 degrees.

Beat eggs lightly. Add all remaining ingredients except for the pecan halves. Mix until well blended. Pour into pie crust shell. Place pie on a cookie sheet. Use the pecan halves to decorate the top of the pie mixture.

Bake for 50-55 minutes until top of filling is set and slightly cracked.

Serve warm or cold with sweetened whipped cream or vanilla ice cream.

## Shopping List

1 unbaked deep dish pie crust shell

1 cup pecan pieces

1/2 cup pecan halves

1/2 cup toffee bits

1/2 cup mini semi-sweet chocolate chips

3 eggs

3 Tbl butter, melted

1/2 cup sugar

1 cup light corn syrup

1 tsp pure vanilla extract

Memphis has Graceland; Nashville has the Grand Ole Opry, but for my money, Tennessee's best bets are natural wonders, like the 800 square mile Great Smoky Mountains National Park. Gatlinburg is a great base of operations for touring the mountains. A little town on the edge of the park, this mecca for artists and crafters has over 100 galleries. A trolley runs the 8-mile loop of shops, restaurants and galleries so you can save your energy for browsing.

Once you make it to the park, it's going to be hard to decide what to do and where to go first. I recommend you make a stop at the Visitor Center in Gatlinburg (or Sevierville if you're visiting Dollywood). There are also four stations within the park, located at the most popular destinations.

For a 100-mile, seven-state view and a sunrise or sunset you'll never forget, head to Clingmans Dome. At 6,684 feet, it's the highest point in the park. Half the ridge is in Tennessee and half is in North Carolina. You can drive to about half-mile below the peak, and then it's a steep hike up, but definitely worth it! The Dome is the highest point along the Appalachian Trail's entire 2,144 mile length.

If it's wildlife you're after, head to Cades Cove. This broad valley surrounded by mountains is the foraging ground of white-tailed deer, black bears, coyotes, ground hogs, turkeys, raccoons and skunks. The Cove is also home to several of the park's nearly one hundred 18th and 19th century churches, cabins and grist mills. An 11-mile loop road that takes you around the entire valley.

Next to the Oconoluftee Visitor Center is the Mountain Farm Museum. Here you can tour a log farmhouse, barn, apple house, springhouse, and a working blacksmith shop. The buildings date from the late 19th century and give a peek at mountain farm life more than 100 years ago.

Every season reveals a different beauty in these mountains. Fall color is spectacular of course, but spring brings the dogwood blossoms, delicate on nearly bare branches, and thunderous waterfalls swollen with newly melted snow— perfectly beautiful.

# Dogwood Cardigan

## Knoxville, Tennessee

*The end of winter in Tennessee is heralded by the return of pink and white dogwood blossoms. Nowhere in the South are the new season and its flowers more celebrated than in Knoxville, with its historic Dogwood Arts Festival. The "Rhythm and Blooms" concerts are a festival highlight. Spread out a blanket and listen to some of the best traditional artists while surrounded by spring bursting into life. Of course a girl needs a gorgeous sweater to hold the evening chill at bay while still drawing attention to her own natural beauty.*

*Thanks to* ***Jinka McLaurin*** *of* ***Loopville*** *in Knoxville, this lovely Dogwood Cardigan with its face framing collar, scooped neckline and body skimming style can't help but make you look taller, slimmer and brighter. You won't want to take it off.*

## About this Project

**Skill Level:** Intermediate

**Finished Sizes:** S (M, L) with finished bust sizes 38 (42, 46)" [97 (107, 117)cm]

**Fit Tip:** Select a size for this sweater that is 2-3" (5-8cm) larger than your actual bust measurement. Olivia is wearing a size Small.

**Project Gauge:** 18 stitches and 24 rows = 4" (10cm) in stockinette stitch on smaller needles; 16 stitches and 22 rows = 4" (10cm) in *Dogwood Lace* pattern on larger needles

## Shopping List

S. Charles Collezione *Sahara* (44% viscose, 36% bamboo, 20% linen, 87 yards/80m); 9 (10, 11) skeins Citrus #05, 2 skeins Natural #1, 1 skein Petal Pink #04

Size US 9 (5.5mm) 24" (60cm) and 40" (100cm) circular needles

Size US 10.5 (6.5mm) 24" (60cm) circular needle

Size J (5.5mm) crochet hook

Button

Tapestry needle

## Stitch Guide

*Dogwood Lace*
Row 1 (RS): *K1, ssk, yo, k5; repeat from * to end.
Row 2 (WS) and all WS rows: Purl.
Row 3: *Ssk, yo, k1, yo, k2tog, k3; repeat from * to end.
Row 5: *K1, ssk, yo, k5; repeat from * to end.
Row 7: Knit.
Row 9: K5, *ssk, yo, k6; repeat from * across, end last repeat k1.
Row 11: K4, *ssk, yo, k1, yo, k2tog, k3; repeat from * across, end last repeat k2.
Row 13: K5, *ssk, yo, k6; repeat from * across, end last repeat k1.
Row 15: Knit.
Row 16: Purl.
Repeat rows 1-16 for pattern.

*Insertion Lace*
Row 1 (RS): With Natural, knit.
Row 2 (WS): Knit.
Row 3: Knit.
Row 4: With Petal Pink, *sl1wyif twice, p4; repeat from * to last 2 stitches, sl1wyif twice.
Row 5: With Petal Pink, sl1wyib twice, *k4, sl1wyib twice; repeat from * to end.
Row 6: With Natural, purl.
Row 7: Purl.
Row 8: Purl.

*Dogwood Lace Chart*

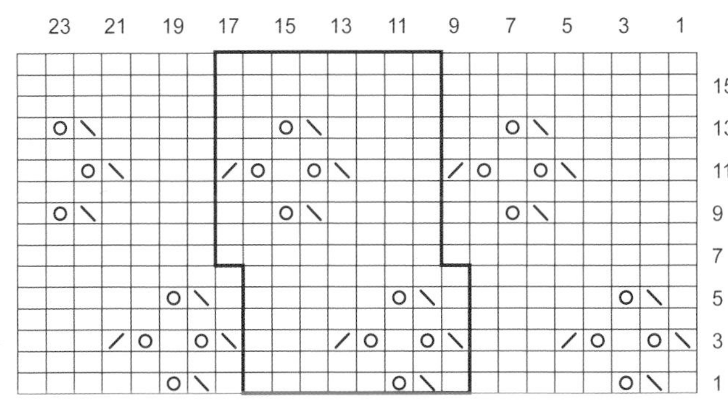


## Instructions

*Back*
Using provisional cast on, larger needles, and Citrus, CO 98 (106, 114) stitches. Work 4 rows stockinette stitch.

*Dogwood Lace section*
Work even in *Dogwood Lace* pattern for two and one-half repeats. (44 rows total have been worked).
Change to smaller needles and Natural. Begin *Insertion Lace* pattern and **at the same time** decrease 18 (20, 22) stitches evenly across first row of pattern. [80 (86, 92) stitches].
After one repeat of *Insertion Lace* pattern, change to Citrus, continuing on smaller needles. Work in stockinette stitch for 12 rows.
*Begin increases*
Next (increase) row (RS): K1, k1f&b, knit to last 2 stitches, k1f&b, k1. Repeat increase row every 6 rows three times. [88 (94, 100) stitches]. Work even for 2 (4, 8) rows or until piece measures 7 (8, 8)" [18 (20, 20)cm] from top edge of *Insertion Lace* pattern. *Note:* If a longer or shorter cardi is desired, make adjustments here.
*Shape armholes*
BO 2 (4, 4) stitches at beginning of next 2 rows. BO 2 stitches at beginning of following 2 rows. [80 (82, 88) stitches].
Next (decrease) row (RS): K1, ssk, knit to last 3 stitches, k2tog, k1.
Next row: Purl.
Repeat last two rows 8 (7, 7) times. [62 (66, 72) stitches]. Work even until armholes measure 7½ (8, 8½)" [19 (20, 22)cm], ending with a WS row and place marker each side of center 28 (30, 34) stitches.

*Shape neck*
Next row (RS): Work across to marker; join second ball of yarn and BO center 28 (30, 34) stitches for back neck; work to end. [17 (18, 19) stitches remain each side for shoulders]. Working both sides at same time, decrease one stitch at each neck edge. [16, (17, 18) stitches remain each side]. Work even until armholes measure 8 (8½, 9)" [20 (22, 23)cm], ending with a WS row.
*Shape shoulders*
BO 4 (5, 6) stitches at beginning of next 2 rows. BO 6 (6, 6) stitches at beginning of next 4 rows.

*Left front*
Using provisional cast on, larger needles, and Citrus, CO 50 (58, 66) stitches. Work 4 rows stockinette stitch.
*Dogwood Lace section*
Work even in *Dogwood Lace* pattern for two and one-half repeats. (44 rows total have been worked).
Change to smaller needles and Natural. Begin *Insertion Lace* pattern and at same time decrease 12 (14, 16) stitches evenly across first row of pattern. [38 (44, 50) stitches]. After one repeat of *Insertion Lace* pattern change to Citrus, continuing on smaller needles. Work in stockinette stitch for 12 rows.
*Begin increases*
Next (increase) row (RS): K1, k1f&b, knit to end. Repeat increase row every 6 rows three times. [42 (48, 54) stitches]. Work even for 2 (4, 8) rows or until piece measures 7 (8, 8)" [18 (20, 20)cm] from top edge of *Insertion Lace* pattern, ending with a WS row. *Note:* If a longer or shorter cardi is desired, make adjustments here.
*Shape armhole*
BO 2 (4, 4) stitches at beginning of next row. BO 2 stitches at beginning of following RS row. [38 (42, 48) stitches].
Next (decrease) row (RS): K1, ssk, knit to end.
Next row: Purl.
Repeat last two rows 8 (7, 7) times. **At the same time**, when armhole measures 1 (1½, 1½)" [2.5 (4, 4)cm], begin neck shaping by decreasing 1 stitch at neck edge every other row 7 (14, 22) times, then every four rows 6 (3, 0) times as follows: work to last 3 stitches, k2tog, k1. [16 (17, 18) stitches]. Work even until piece measures same as back to start of shoulder shaping, ending with a WS row.
*Shape shoulder*
BO 4 (5, 6) stitches at beginning of next row. BO 6 (6, 6) stitches at beginning of next two RS rows.

*Right front*
Work as for left front, reversing shaping.

*Sleeves*
Using crochet cast on, larger needles, and Petal Pink, CO 58 (58, 60) stitches. Knit one row. Purl one row. Change to Citrus. Work 2 rows stockinette stitch.
Next row (RS): K1 (1, 2), work row 1 of *Dogwood Lace* pattern, end k1 (1, 2). Continue working for one repeat of *Dogwood Lace*, keeping first and last 1 (1, 2) stitches in stockinette stitch. Change to smaller needles and Natural. Begin *Insertion Lace* pattern and **at the same time** decrease 8 (8, 10) stitches evenly across first row of pattern. [50 (50, 50) stitches]. After one repeat of *Insertion Lace* pattern change to Citrus, continuing on smaller needles. Work in stockinette stitch for 4 rows.
*Begin increases*
Next (increase) row (RS): K1, m1, knit to last stitch, m1, k1. Repeat increase row every 6 (6, 4) rows 7 (9, 11) times. [66 (70, 74) stitches]. Work even until piece measures 11½ (12, 13)" [29 (30, 33)cm] from cast on edge, ending with a WS row.

*Jinka McLaurin*, the designer of this lovely cardi, owns *Loopville* in Knoxville, Tennessee. If you're in town, stop by for tea and knitting. You can find *Loopville* online at LoopvilleYarn.com and on Facebook as Loopville.

*Shape cap*
BO 2 (4, 4) stitches at beginning of next 2 rows. BO 2 stitches at beginning of next 2 rows, then decrease 1 stitch at each end of RS rows until 48 (52, 54) stitches remain. Work even until cap measures 2¾ (3¼, 3¾)" [7 (8, 10)cm] from beginning of cap shaping. BO all stitches.

## Finishing

Block pieces according to chart on page 150. Sew shoulder seams. Set in sleeves, sew sleeve and side seams, matching pattern rows carefully.

*Collar*
With smaller needles and Natural, cast on 90 (92, 94) stitches. Knit one row. Purl one row.
Next row (RS): K1f&b into every stitch. [180 (184, 188) stitches]. Continue in stockinette stitch for 8 rows. Change to Petal Pink. Knit 1 row. Purl 1 row. BO all stitches very loosely. Sew collar to neck edge.

*Sweater body edging*
On right front side below collar, with larger needles and Petal Pink, pick up and knit three of every four stitches around to the bottom edge; remove provisional cast on and knit the live stitches, continuing to left front edge, then pick up and knit three out of every four stitches to below collar. Purl one row. BO all stitches loosely. Crochet a chain button loop and sew on button at neck edge.
Weave in ends.

# Bears & Blooms Hat

Sevierville, Tennessee

*Spring in the mountains around Sevierville brings the return of two things— black bears and wildflowers. Blooms and bears can be found both on this precious hat and while hiking the Appalachian Trail, more than 70 miles of which crosses nearby Great Smoky Mountains National Park. Black bears feature prominently in the area folklore. We especially like the tale that all the black bears gather once a year in a secret cave for food, music and dancing. If we were invited, we'd wear a hat like this!*

*Although an advanced project, this hat by designer* **Ava Lynn Green** *is a good first stranded knitting project suitable for an adventurous beginner. The black and winter white are stranded on a section of hat without increases or decreases, and the remaining color work is embroidered on after the hat is knitted. Not a fan of Fair Isle? Knit the whole thing in winter white and embroider on the bears as well. Any way you make it, this hat will be adorable.*

## About this Project

**Skill Level:** Advanced

**Finished Size:** One size. Fits head 20-24" (50-60cm) in circumference

**Project Gauge:** 21 stitches and 25 rows = 4" (10cm) in stockinette stitch on larger needles with *Classic Wool*

## Shopping List

Patons *Classic Wool* (100% merino wool, 223 yards/204m); 1 skein each Winter White #201, Black #226, Leaf Green #240

DMC *Tapestry Wool* (100% wool, 8.7 yards/8m); 1 skein each Light Blue #7031, Gray #7282, Tan #7453

Size US 6 (4mm) 16" (40cm) circular needle

Size US 7 (4.5mm) 16" (40cm) circular needle

Size US 7 (4.5mm) double pointed needles

Stitch markers

Stitch holder

Tapestry needle

8 brown beads

4 orange 20mm flower buttons (buttons shown by Dill Buttons of America #280865)

Sewing needle and thread

## Instructions

With smaller circular needle and *Classic Wool* Winter White, CO 98 stitches; place marker and join for working in the round, being careful not to twist stitches.
Round 1-14: Knit.
Round 15: Knit, increasing 10 stitches evenly around. (108 stitches)
Round 16-19: Change to larger circular needle. Knit.
Round 20-43: Join *Classic Wool* Black and continue in stranded color work technique. Beginning with chart A, work the first row of the graph from right to left, repeating the chart four times around. Work each subsequent row in the same manner, from right to left. Cut *Classic Wool* Black, leaving 8" (20cm) tail.
Round 44-48: Continue with *Classic Wool* Winter White only. Knit.
Round 49: *Ssk, k8, k2tog; repeat from * nine times. (90 stitches)
Round 50: Knit.
Round 51: *Ssk, k6, k2tog; repeat from * nine times. (72 stitches)
Round 52: Knit.
Round 53: *Ssk, k4, k2tog; repeat from * nine times. (54 stitches)
Round 54: Knit, changing to double pointed needles.
Round 55: *Ssk, k2, k2tog; repeat from * nine times. (36 stitches)
Round 56: Knit.
Round 57: *Ssk, k2tog; repeat from * nine times. (18 stitches)
Round 58-60: Knit.
Do not cut the yarn.

## Finishing

*Top trim*
Place the first six stitches on one double pointed needle. Place the other stitches on a holder. Continuing with *Classic Wool* Winter White, work 4" (10cm) of I-cord with the first six stitches. When cord measures 4" (10cm), k2tog two times, pass the first k2tog decrease over the second, k2tog again and pass the second decrease over the third. Cut yarn, leaving an 8" (20cm) tail. Pull tail through remaining loop to fasten. Move the next six stitches from the holder to a double pointed needle and join *Classic*

Artist and designer *Ava Lynne Green* owns *Terri's Yarns and Crafts* in Sevierville, Tennessee. In addition to knit and crochet, she designs for cross-stitch and needlepoint and is an accomplished painter. Find her online at TerrisYarnsAndCrafts.com.

*Wool* Leaf Green. Work 4" (10cm) of I-cord and finish as with *Classic Wool* Winter White. Move the last six stitches from the holder to a double pointed needle and join *Classic Wool* Black. Work 4" (10cm) of I-cord and finish as with *Classic Wool* Winter White. To make the topknot, cross the black cord over the green and under the white. Bring the white under the green. Bring the green under the black. Fold the bound off edges to the base of the topknot and use the long tails to stitch them in place.

*Duplicate stitch and embroidery*

Using the colored boxes on chart B for placement, duplicate stitch the mountains with DMC Light Blue, the grass with *Classic Wool* Leaf Green, and the muzzle with DMC Tan and Gray. Stitch the beads on each bear for eyes where the half circles appear on chart B. Use outline stitch and lazy daisy stitches for stems and leaves between each bear, using photo as a guide. Stitch the flower buttons on the top of each stem. Weave in ends.

Chart A

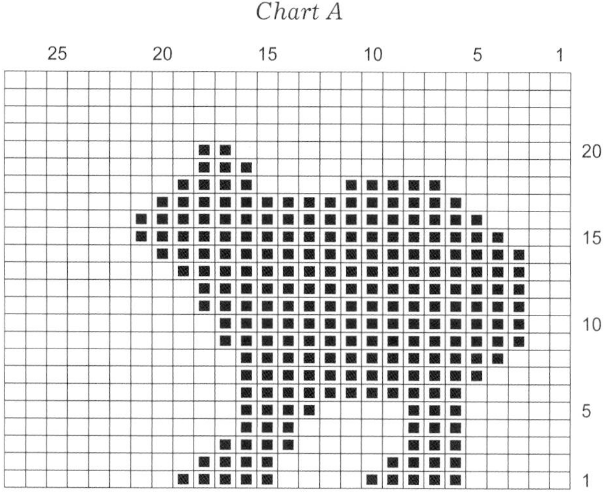


Chart B

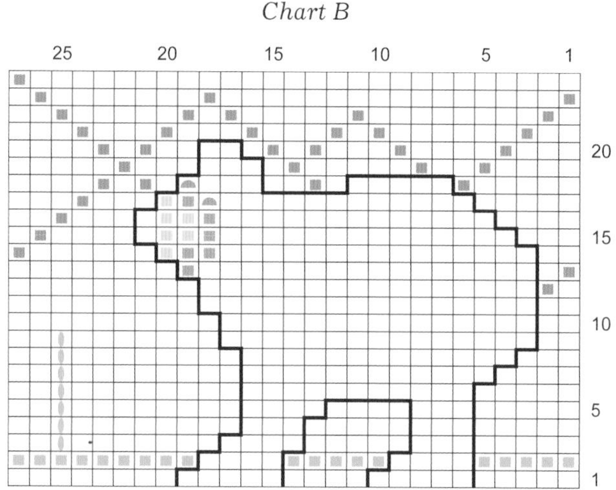

# Pecan Divinity

*Fluffy divinity and sweet pecans, this confection is definitely heavenly. Don't attempt this dessert in high humidity unless the air conditioner is running, or you'll have a divinely sticky mess.*

## Directions

*Tip:* This recipe works best with a stand mixer. If you have a hand mixer, press a friend into service to continue the beating after the addition of the first half of the boiling sugar syrup. Promise them the bowl and beater and you'll have plenty of volunteers! Also, if it's humid and/or raining, close the windows and turn on the air conditioning or heater as divinity needs a dry room to set up best.

Line an 8"x8" square pan with waxed paper.

Mix corn syrup, sugar, salt and water in saucepan. Cook over medium heat, stirring, until sugar is dissolved. Continue cooking, without stirring, increasing heat as needed to reach 248 degrees on a candy thermometer, or until a small amount of mixture forms a firm ball when dropped in cold water.

Meanwhile, beat egg whites until stiff, but not dry. Pour about half the syrup slowly over whites, beating constantly. Return the remaining syrup to the stove and cook without stirring until a small amount forms hard threads in cold water (272 degrees on a candy thermometer). Add slowly to first egg white/syrup mixture— which your buddy or stand mixer has been beating the entire time— and beat until mixture holds its shape like thick marshmallow cream. Fold in vanilla extract and pecan pieces. Quickly scoop into a waxed paper lined pan. Pat flat, but don't compress. Allow to cool and dry (except the stuff on the beater and left in the mixing bowl which are for you to sample now).

When completely cool and dry, cut into 1" squares using a very sharp knife dipped in hot water and quickly dried on a towel. Store in airtight container with layers of waxed paper in between to prevent sticking.

## Shopping List

- 1/2 cup light corn syrup
- 2 1/2 cups granulated sugar
- 1/4 tsp salt
- 1/2 cup water
- 2 egg whites
- 1 tsp vanilla extract
- 1 cup pecans, chopped medium-fine

The Ozark Mountains are renowned for their unspoiled forests, and beautiful lakes and rivers. The largely rural area around Fayetteville is home to sprawling farms and ranches carved out of the gorgeous Arkansas wilderness, surrounded by rugged mountains.

There's a fascinating and beautiful world below the surface of the mountains. The Ozarks are full of thousands of limestone caves, with eight privately owned caves open to the public. Blanchard Springs Caverns, in Mountain View, is operated by the U.S. Forest Service and offers guided tours through two of the three levels of a huge living cavern system. The upper level's Dripstone Trail is a fantasy land of calcite formations, with everything from hollow soda straws to huge stalagmites. One of these rooms, which were part of the sea 350 million years ago, is the size of three football fields!

Most of Arkansas' caves are wild, meaning they have not been adapted for the average tourist. For those who are physically fit and up to the challenge, guided wild cave tours are available at several locations. At Blanchard, you could take a 4 hour tour along steep slopes, crawling on hands and knees through mud and clay, wearing a hardhat, knee pads and gloves. Or you could just stroll the one hour Dripstone Trail tour and then go shopping for Ozark handcrafts in Mountain View. It's up to you....

If you're a cave-man or woman, don't miss Cosmic Caverns with its underground lake and bridge, Hurricane River Cave with a waterfall at its entrance, Mystic Caverns with its 28 foot "pipe organ" formation, or the Old Spanish Treasure Cave with its ancient sea fossils. Still can't get enough of caves? You can sleep in one at the Beckham Creek Cave Lodge. With a 2,000 square foot living room, full kitchen and 5 bedrooms, you can host an unforgettable family reunion in a living, ever-changing cavern.

From its first European settlers to the Civil War, the South has been formed and re-formed by the history of its people. In Arkansas, history has marked the land itself, with the story of millions of years etched under the ground.

# Ozark Mountain Vest

## Mountain View, Arkansas

*Southern mountain ranges each have their own natural palette— blues and grays of the Smokies, blues and greens of the Blue Ridge, and the browns and greens of the Ozarks. Arkansas isn't called the Natural State for nothing and the breathtaking natural landscapes make the state a magnet for those who love the great outdoors.*

*Mountain View, Arkansas is a great place to visit with the Folk Art Center, bluegrass festivals and fantastic views. Nearby are the Blanchard Caverns, the inspiration for this ruggedly handsome vest. With its colorway inspired by the Ozarks themselves, the texture in the sections, created by strategically placed reverse stockinette stitches, is a nod to the craggy stalactites. Easy-fitting and an easy knit with a wide range of sizes, you can knit one for the man in your life and one for yourself while you're at it!*

## About this Project

**Skill Level:** Easy

**Finished Sizes:** XS (S, M, L, XL, 2X, 3X, 4X) with finished chest sizes 42¼ (44½, 45¾, 49, 51¼, 53½, 55¾, 58¼)" [107 (113, 116, 125, 130, 136, 142, 148)cm]

**Fit Tip:** This vest is designed with a relaxed fit to be worn with about 4-6" (10-15cm) of ease. Choose a finished size at least 4" (10cm) larger than your chest measurement. Cavan is wearing a size Medium with a finished measurement of 45¾" (116cm).

**Project Gauge:** 18 stitches and 24 rows = 4" (10cm) in stockinette stitch on larger needles

### Shopping List

Lorna's Laces *Shepherd Worsted* (100% superwash wool, 225 yards/205m); 2 (3, 3, 3, 3, 3, 3, 3) skeins Solitude (MC) and 1 skein Fiddlehead (CC)

Size US 6 (4mm) straight and 16" (40cm) circular needles

Size US 7 (4.5mm) needles

Stitch marker

Tapestry needle

## Instructions

*Back*

With MC and smaller needles, CO 90 (94, 100, 104, 108, 112, 118, 122) stitches. Work in 1x1 ribbing for 8 rows. Change to CC and work in 1x1 ribbing for 1 row more, then change to MC and work in 1x1 ribbing for 5 rows more (14 rows total). Change to larger needles. With MC, work even in stockinette stitch until piece measures 15 (15, 15½, 15½, 16, 16, 16½, 17)" [38 (38, 39, 39, 41, 41, 42, 43)cm] from beginning, ending with a WS row.

*Shape armholes*

BO 5 (5, 6, 6, 7, 7, 8, 9) stitches at beginning of next 2 rows. Decrease 1 stitch each end of every RS row 8 (9, 9, 10, 10, 11, 12, 12) times. [64 (66, 70, 72, 74, 76, 78, 80) stitches. Work even in stockinette stitch until armholes measure 10 (10½, 10½, 11, 11, 11½, 11½, 12)" [25 (27, 27, 28, 28, 29, 29, 30)cm], ending with a WS row.

*Shape shoulders and back neck*

Mark center 30 (30, 32, 32, 32, 32, 34, 36) stitches. BO 4 (4, 5, 5, 5, 6, 6, 6) stitches at beginning of row. Knit to center 30 (30, 32, 32, 32, 32, 34, 36) stitches, join a second ball of yarn and BO center 30 (30, 32, 32, 32, 32, 34, 36) stitches, knit to end. Working both sides separately at the same time, BO 4 (4, 5, 5, 5, 6, 6, 6) stitches at beginning of next row, purl to end. BO 4 (5, 5, 5, 6, 6, 6, 6) stitches at beginning of next 2 rows, then BO 5 (5, 5, 6, 6, 6, 6, 6) stitches at beginning of following 2 rows; and, **at the same time** decrease 1 stitch at each neck edge every row 4 times. [13 (14, 15, 16, 17, 18, 18, 18) stitches each side].

*Front*

*Note:* When working stripes in CC, work color sections of CC that match MC in reverse stockinette stitch for texture.

Work as for back until armholes measure 1 (1, 1, 1½, 1½, 1½, 1½, 2)" [2.5 (2.5, 2.5, 4, 4, 4, 4, 5)cm], **at the same time** working in stripe pattern as follows:

Ribbing: Work as for back.

Body: 10 rows MC, 12 rows CC, *8 rows MC, 12 rows CC; repeat from * until one full CC stripe after beginning of neck shaping has been worked; work remainder of front in MC.

I think the Ozarks are at their best in fall, when the changing leaves bring out the browns and greens of the mountains and streams— Mother Nature at her colorful best. The air is crisp and leaves rustle underfoot. It's a magical time in the Ozarks.

*Shape neck*
When armholes measure 1 (1, 1, 1½, 1½, 1½, 1½, 2)" [2.5 (2.5, 2.5, 4, 4, 4, 4, 5)cm], ending with a WS row, begin neck shaping (continue armhole shaping as set until complete). Next row (RS): Work in pattern to center 2 stitches, join a second ball of yarn and BO center 2 stitches, work in pattern to end. Decrease 1 stitch each neck edge every other row 10 (10, 11, 11, 11, 11, 12, 13) times, then every 4th row 8 times. [13 (14, 15, 16, 17, 18, 18, 18) stitches each side]. Work even until piece measures same as back to start of shoulder shaping.
*Shape shoulders*
BO 4 (4, 5, 5, 5, 6, 6, 6) stitches at beginning of next 2 rows.
BO 4 (5, 5, 5, 6, 6, 6, 6) stitches at beginning of following 2 rows.
BO 5 (5, 5, 6, 6, 6, 6, 6) stitches at beginning of next 2 rows.

## Finishing

Weave in ends. Block according to chart on page 151.
Sew shoulder and side seams.

*Neck trim*
With smaller circular needle, RS facing, and MC, pick up and knit 142 (146, 146, 146, 150, 152, 154) stitches around neck opening, starting at point of v-neck. Do not join, work back and forth in rows. Work in 1x1 ribbing for 6 rows. Change to CC and work in 1x1 ribbing for 1 row more. Change to MC and work in 1x1 ribbing for 2 rows more. BO in rib. Lap edges as shown and sew in place.

*Armhole trim*
With smaller circular needle, RS facing, and MC, pick up and knit 100 (104, 104, 108, 108, 112, 112, 116) stitches around armhole opening. Place marker and join for working in the round. Work in 1x1 ribbing following same color pattern as neck trim. BO in rib.

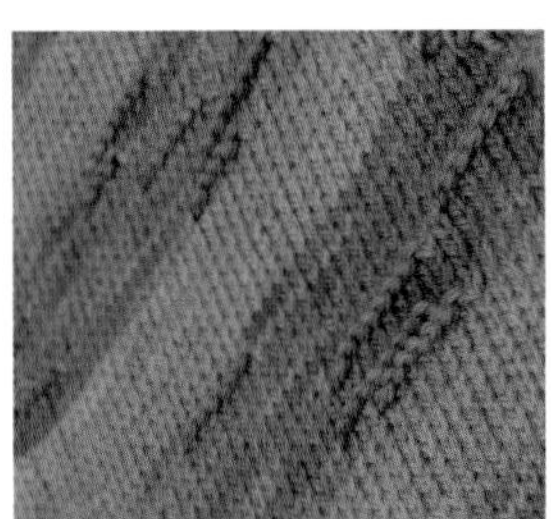

The rustic texture is created by working selected stitches in reverse stockinette stitch.

## Tips

- We picked out the brown for the reverse stockinette stitches, but you could select any of the colors in the yarn, or even randomly select groups of stitches to create the textural interest.
- If you'd like a much slimmer fit, you can choose a size 2" (5cm) larger than your chest measurement. For a flattering fit, resist the urge to knit a size less than 2" (5cm) larger than your chest measurement.

## Arkansas Southwest Trail

The State of Arkansas is crisscrossed with "Heritage Trails," history trips that tell the stories of the state, from pre-Pony Express days and through the Civil War. The trails are a chance to re-live important historical events that shaped not only Arkansas, but the country as well. The famous Southwest Trail starts in St. Louis, Missouri and ends in Texas' Red River Valley. Originally a dirt path pre-1820, it became the primary migration route West. By the 1830s more than 80% of Arkansas' population had found their new homes traveling this route. The trail winds through the Ozarks and some of the state's best vacation spots. Here are some highlights along the way:

*Washington* - Part town and part living history museum, the entire town is designated as a state park and is on the National Register of Historic Places. Home to less than 150 people, Washington serves as an educational site. Daily programs with costumed interpreters and more than thirty restored historic buildings depict life in the town from 1824 to 1889.

*North Little Rock* - "Gone with the Wind" fans won't want to miss the Old Mill, an authentic reproduction of a water-powered grist mill that was featured in the opening scene. The Cherokee Trail of Tears, a route of forced migration, passes through North Little Rock and is commemorated with interpretive panels along the North Shore Riverwalk.

*Batesville* - This small town boasts architecture representing every decade from 1840 to the present, with two historic districts showcasing a beautiful collection of grand Victorian homes.

*Pocahontas* - In addition to its Victorian Italianate courthouse built in 1872, the lovingly restored square is home to fine restaurants and shopping. The county has five rivers and a lake, and boasts excellent canoeing and big-bass fishing.

*Maynard* - The Maynard Pioneer Museum is built around a 19th century log cabin saved from demolition and carefully reassembled in its present location. The cabin is outfitted with period furnishings and artifacts representing rural family life in the 1800s.

# Farmer's Market Skirt

Fayetteville, Arkansas

*In the South, we love our jeans, at least in the cooler months. During the stickier summer months, wearing jeans feels something like being swaddled in plastic wrap from waist to ankles and then stepping into a steam room. What your legs wouldn't give for a cooling breeze. Hiding indoors with air conditioning is an option, but if you're visiting Fayetteville in summer, you'll want to enjoy the outdoor Farmer's Market, the Botanical Garden of the Ozarks, and maybe do a bit of antiquing. Did someone mention yarn shopping?*

*So if you're a stylish denim-loving girl, summer travel in the South means skirts, like this reverse stockinette beauty from* ***Sarah Jo Burch*** *and* ***Handheld Knitting****. Knit in Rowan's Denim yarn, it will fade and soften with every wearing, just like your favorite jeans. You can adjust the length to your liking, and go as modest or as bare as you dare. Either way, your legs will thank you.*

## About this Project

**Skill Level:** Easy-mediate

**Finished Sizes:** XS (S, M, L, XL) with finished hip sizes 34 (36, 40, 44, 48)" [86 (91, 102, 112, 122)cm]

**Fit Tip:** Select size based on hip measurement. Olivia is wearing the Extra Small size, knit 2" (5cm) shorter than the standard pattern length.

**Project Gauge:** 20 stitches and 28 rows = 4" (10cm) in stockinette stitch *before* washing and drying

### Shopping List

Rowan *Denim* (100% cotton, 102 yards/93m); 7 (9, 11, 12, 14) skeins Nashville #225 (MC), 3 (4, 4, 5, 6) skeins Ecru #324 (CC)

Size US 6 (4mm) 32" (80cm) circular needle

Size G (4mm) crochet hook (for crochet trim version, shown)

Stitch markers

Tapestry needle

1¼" (3cm) wide elastic in length of waist measurement

Large safety pin

## Instructions

With MC, CO 168 (180, 204, 216, 240) stitches, placing marker every 14 (15, 17, 18, 20) stitches. Place uniquely colored marker to mark beginning of round (count as marker 12) and join, being careful not to twist stitches.

*Waistband*

Round 1: Knit. Repeat this round until piece measures 1½" (4cm).

Next round: Purl (turning round made).

Repeat round 1 for 1½" (4cm) more.

*Main skirt*

Round 1: *Sl1wyif; knit to next marker, slip marker; repeat from * to end of round.

Round 2: *P1, knit to next marker, slip marker; repeat from * to end of round.

Round 3-8: Repeat rounds 1-2 three times.

Round 9: Repeat round 1.

Round 10: *P1, knit to next marker, remove marker, m1, replace marker, sl1wyif, m1, knit to next marker, slip marker; repeat from * to end of round. (12 stitches increased; 1 on each side of markers 1, 3, 5, 7, 9 and 11)

Repeat rounds 1-10 for pattern until there are 50 (55, 60, 65, 70) pattern rows and piece measures approximately 7 (8, 8½, 9½, 10)" [18 (20, 21, 23, 25)cm] from end of waistband.

*Note:* This pattern will create 12 seam-like columns of slipped stitches visible on the reverse stockinette side of the piece.

*Waist to low hip*

Remove markers 2, 4, 6, 8 and 10 (keep end of round marker in place) and continue in pattern, slipping, purling and increasing at each side of markers 1, 3, 5, 7, 9 and 11 as before. Do not slip or increase at the marker that denotes the beginning of the round (marker 12).

*Note:* At this point, there will only be 6 seam-like columns of slipped stitches visible on the reverse stockinette side of the piece.

*Low hip to bottom edge*

Continue in pattern as set until piece measures 162 (174, 190, 201, 217) rows or approximately 23 (25, 27, 29, 31)" [58 (63, 68, 74, 79)cm] from end of waistband, or desired length.

*Note:* If you decide to adjust the length of the skirt, keep in mind that for every 5" (13cm) in length you knit, you will lose 1" (2.5cm) as it shrinks in the wash.

*Sarah Jo Burch* lives in Fayetteville, Arkansas. You can follow her at SarahJoKnits.blogspot.com. *Handheld Knitting* is located in the historic downtown area of Fayetteville. You can also find the shop online at HandheldKnitting.com.

*Bottom trim (crochet version as shown)*
Change to CC and knit back and forth, rather than in the round, knitting every row in garter stitch, for 2" (5cm). BO until one loop remains on needle. Change to crochet hook.
*Begin crochet lace section*
With CC, work one single crochet in each bound off stitch across bottom edge.
Row 1: Ch 4, skip 1, *dc in next stitch, ch 1, skip 1; repeat from * to end.
Row 2: Ch 1, *work 2 sc in next ch-1 space; repeat from * to end.
Row 3-6: Repeat rows 1-2 two times. Tie off.

*Alternate knitted trim version (not shown)*
Change to CC, knit back and forth, not in the round, knitting every row in garter stitch, for 2" (5cm). Do not bind off.

*Begin lace section*
Row 1: *K2tog, yo; repeat from * to end.
Row 2: Knit.
Row 3-22: Repeat rows 1-2 ten times. BO knitwise.

## Finishing

Machine wash and dry skirt and a butterfly of enough MC to seam waistband. Because the darker yarn will release color, use a color catching laundry aid for the first few washes. Fold waistband in half along turning round to stockinette side (will be wrong side on finished skirt) to form casing for elastic. Whipstitch closed, leaving 1½" (4cm) opening to insert elastic. Cut elastic 1" (2.5cm) longer than waist measurement with elastic lightly stretched. Put a large safety pin in one end of elastic. Insert pin and elastic in opening of waistband. Use pin to push elastic through casing, careful not to twist elastic. Overlap elastic ends by 1" (2.5cm) and securely stitch through both thicknesses. Tuck inside waistband and whipstitch remaining opening closed. Weave in ends on smooth side (WS) of skirt.

## Tips

- Rowan *Denim* is surface dyed, so some dye will come off while knitting. Probably best not to knit this project while wearing white pants or your favorite cashmere sweater.
- This yarn shrinks in the first washing and drying. You'll lose about 20% of the length (but not width) in the wash. Keep this in mind if you substitute yarn.
- Wind a butterfly of enough yarn to sew up the casing and wash it at the same time as the skirt so the excess dye will wash out and the yarn used for sewing up will preshrink.
- For a shorter or longer waist-to-hip length to customize the silhouette to work for your figure, work the waist to hip section in increments of five rows, making sure to stay in pattern every 10 rows, and then adjusting stitch markers for the next section. Work skirt to desired length.

# Whipped Maple Candy

*Maple syrup— it's not just for breakfast anymore! Arkansas' Ozark maple trees produce a deliciously sweet syrup, which is all you need, along with some heat and a strong stirring arm, to create melt-in-your-mouth and highly addictive maple candy. Trees never tasted so good.*

## Directions

Line an 8"x8" pan with waxed paper or, if using candy molds, spray lightly with non-stick spray. Pour syrup into a heavy 4 quart saucepan. Bring the syrup to a boil over medium-high heat, stirring occasionally. Lower to medium temperature. Boil until the syrup reaches 235 degrees on a candy thermometer. Remove the pan from the heat. Allow the syrup to cool to 175 degrees without stirring, about 15-20 minutes.

With a wooden spoon, beat the syrup rapidly until the syrup becomes thick and the color turns light. Pour the syrup into the lined pan or into candy molds. Allow to cool completely at room temperature.

Unmold, or using a sharp knife dipped in hot water, cut into 25 squares. Store between layers of waxed paper away from heat in an airtight container. Keeps up to one month.

Makes 18-25 pieces.

## Shopping List

3 cups pure maple syrup

What is it about Louisiana that captures the imagination of so many writers and filmmakers? I think it might be that silky French Creole accent— think Dennis Quaid in "The Big Easy." Whatever it is, anyone who's visited Louisiana knows how quickly the place can seduce you.

Of course, everyone's familiar with New Orleans, party central 365 days a year! Its active nightlife and semi-spooky gothic architecture make the city a perfect setting for vampire tales, like those by Anne Rice and Charlaine Harris.

In the "Crescent City," phenomenal food is almost as famous as the city itself is. Lighter-than-air beignets and dark chicory coffee at Café du Monde are a must for any visitor. Celebrity chef Emeril Lagasse's career began here, and three of his restaurants are "peppered" throughout the city. After a great dinner, try Bananas Foster for dessert. It was invented at Brennan's, an iconic French Quarter restaurant since 1946, and is a great stop on any tourist's quest to eat her way through New Orleans.

Music is a large part of Louisiana's culture, and the birthplace of jazz, America's only indigenous form of music. New Orleans is still the best place in the world to hear it, whether you're listening to street performers, Dixieland jazz bands on parade, or world-famous musicians in French Quarter nightclubs.

Bayou country is the home of Zydeco. With its fiddles and accordions, it combines Cajun music with rhythm and blues. Zydeco's irresistible energy will get even the shyest wallflowers out on the dance floor, or at least tapping their toes. And after all that Cajun cookin' it probably wouldn't hurt to burn off a few calories.

Louisiana's nickname is "Sportsman's Paradise," and on this front it doesn't disappoint. Thousands of miles of hiking and biking trails, bayous to canoe and kayak, unrivaled bird watching and sport fishing are just a few of the options available to outdoors enthusiasts.

Come with us to Louisiana, and prepare to be seduced!

# *Sunshine Sweater*

Lacombe, Louisiana

*There's something about wearing lighter colors in the summer that just makes you feel cooler. Sure, chic big-city black is fine for the folks in Manhattan, but step in the blazing southern sun wearing that inky shade and even a lady will quickly find herself, well ... schvitzing! So distressing, it's a lesson you won't need to learn twice.*

*This cottony sweater is designed in the ultimate summer color, sunshine yellow. Knit in the round to the underarms, there's very little finishing work. Hurray! Textural interest comes from the seed stitch bands and saddle shoulders. Designers* ***Carolyn Hughes*** *and* ***Pam McNeely*** *of* ***McNeedles*** *in Lacombe, Louisiana have thankfully provided natural air conditioning as well as a feminine touch with the lacy inset. This top is beaming with Louisiana pride, so much we can't help but sing the state song. All together now: "You are my sunshine, my only sunshine...."*

## About this Project

**Skill Level:** Intermediate

**Finished Sizes:** S (M, L, XL) with finished bust sizes 35 (38, 41½, 45)" [89 (97, 105, 114)cm]

**Fit:** This sweater is designed to be worn with moderate ease. Choose a finished bust size 2-4" (5-10cm) larger than your actual bust size. Olivia is wearing a size Small.

**Project Gauge:** 20 stitches and 28 rows = 4" (10cm) in stockinette stitch on larger needle

### Shopping List

Cascade *Sierra Quatro* (80% Pima cotton, 20% wool, 191 yards/174m); 5 (6, 6, 7) skeins Butterscotch #92

Size US 5 (3.75mm) 24" (60cm) circular needle

Size US 6 (4mm) 16" (40cm) and 24" (60cm) circular needles

Stitch markers

Tapestry needle

## Stitch Guide

*Seed Stitch (worked in round on an even number of stitches)*
Round 1: *K1, p1; repeat from * around.
Round 2: *P1, k1; repeat from * around.
Repeat rounds 1-2 until desired length.

*Seed Stitch (worked in rows on an even number of stitches)*
Row 1: *K1, p1; repeat from * to end.
Row 2: *P1, k1; repeat from * to end.
Repeat rows 1-2 until desired length.

*Eyelet Ridge*
Row 1 (WS): Purl.
Row 2 (RS): *K2tog, yo; repeat from * to end.

*Sunshine Lace (worked in the round in multiples of 8)*
Round 1 and 3: *K1, p1; repeat from * to end.
Round 2 and 4: *P1, k1; repeat from * to end.
Round 5: *K1, yo, ssk, k3, k2tog, yo; repeat from * to end.
Round 6: Knit.
Round 7: *K2, yo, ssk, k1, k2tog, yo, k1; repeat from * to end.
Round 8: Knit.
Round 9: *K3, yo, sk2p, yo, k2; repeat from * to end.
Round 10: Knit.
Round 11-14: Repeat rounds 1-4.
Round 15: *K3, yo, sk2p, yo, k2; repeat from * to end.
Round 16: Knit.
Round 17: *K2, yo, k2tog, k1, ssk, yo, k1; repeat from * to end.
Round 18: Knit.
Round 19: *K1, yo, k2tog, k3, ssk, yo; repeat from * to end.
Round 20: Knit.
Round 21-24: Repeat rounds 1-4.

## Instructions

*Shoulder Saddles (make 2)*
With larger needles, CO 10 (13, 13, 15) stitches. Work in *Seed Stitch* until piece measures 3 (3½, 3¾, 4)" [8 (9, 9.5, 10)cm]. BO.

*Body*
With smaller needle, CO 88 (96, 104, 112) stitches, place marker, CO 88 (96, 104, 112) stitches, place unique marker at beginning of round. Join for working in the round, being careful not to twist stitches. [176 (192, 208, 224) stitches]. Work in *Seed Stitch* for 4 rounds. Change to larger needle. Work even in stockinette stitch until piece measures 4" (10cm) from beginning. Begin *Sunshine Lace* pattern, working rounds 1-24 once. Work even in stockinette stitch until piece measures 10½" (11, 12, 13)" [27 (28, 30, 33)cm].

*Back*
*Shape armholes*
Place next 88 (96, 104, 112) stitches on hold for front. Working back and forth in rows, continue on 88 (96, 104, 112) back stitches as follows:
BO 3 (4, 5, 6) stitches at beginning of next 2 rows. Decrease 1 stitch each side every other row 3 (4, 5, 6) times as follows: k1, ssk; knit to 3 stitches before end of row, k2tog, k1. [76 (80, 84, 88) stitches]. Work even in stockinette stitch until back measures 17 (17½, 18½, 19½)" [43 (44, 47, 49.5)cm]. BO 15 (17, 19, 20) stitches at beginning of next 2 rows and BO remaining 46 (46, 46, 48) back neck stitches.

*Front*
Work as for back, including armhole shaping, until piece measures 15½ (16, 17, 17½)" [40 (41, 43, 44.5)cm].
*Shape neck*
Next row (RS): Knit to center 24 (24, 24, 26) stitches, join new yarn and BO center 24 (24, 24, 26) stitches, work to end of row. [26 (28, 30, 31) stitches on each side]. Working both sides separately at the same time, decrease 1 stitch each neck edge every row 11 times. [15 (17, 19, 20) stitches]. Work even until front measures same as back. BO 15 (17, 19, 20) shoulder stitches.

*Sunshine Lace Chart*

knit
purl
yarnover
ssk
k2tog
sk2p

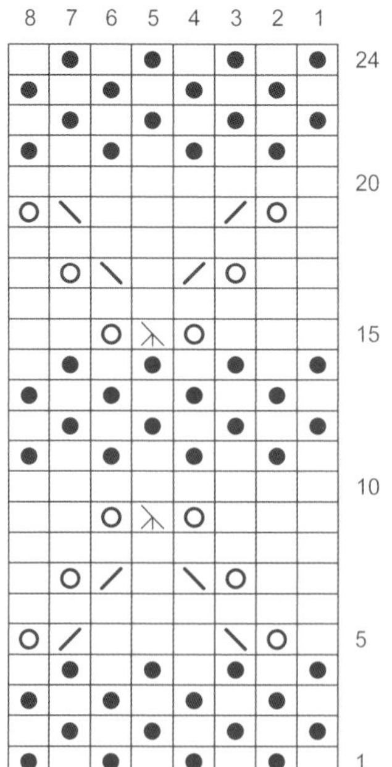

## Finishing

Weave in ends. Block body and saddles to measurements in blocking table on page 153.

*Saddles*
Sew saddles to front and back shoulder seams using mattress stitch.

*Neck finishing*
With smaller needle and RS facing, pick up and knit 46 (46, 46, 48) back neck stitches, 10 (13, 13, 15) stitches along end of saddle, 7 stitches along neck shaping, 24 (24, 24, 26) front neck stitches, 7 stitches along neck shaping, and 10 (13, 13, 15) stitches along end of opposite saddle. [104 (110, 110, 118) stitches]. Do not join; work back and forth in rows. Work both rows of *Eyelet Ridge* pattern. BO kwise on WS. Sew side of neck trim closed.

*Sleeves*
With larger 16" (40cm) needle, starting at underarm edge, pick up and knit 74 (78, 82, 86) stitches around armhole opening. Place marker and join for working in the round. Working in stockinette stitch, knit 2 rounds. Decrease 1 stitch each end of round every other round twice, then every 4th round five times, then every other round twice as follows: K1, ssk, knit to last 3 stitches, k2tog, k1. [56 (60, 64, 68) stitches]. Work even until sleeve measures 5 (5½, 6, 6½)" [13 (14, 15, 16.5)cm]. Work 6 rounds of *Seed Stitch*. BO loosely in pattern.
Weave in remaining ends and block sleeves according to table.

*Pam McNeely's* shop is located in a quaint country style building in Lacombe, Lousiana, a short 45 minute drive from New Orleans. You can find *McNeedles* online at McNeedles-LA.com.

# Morning After Scarflet

Bon Temps, Louisiana

*The sticky, sweaty (and very sexy) fictional Louisiana town of Bon Temps is home to author Charlaine Harris' characters Sookie Stackhouse and her on-again, off-again boyfriend, Vampire Bill. We all know that a Southern lady is nothing if not discreet about her love life, so a vampire-dating girl needs a little something to camouflage the bite marks after a night of passion. Silk scarves might work for Yankee girls, but not in the Deep South— especially when it's so hot outside you could pull a baked potato right out of the ground. This Morning After Scarflet, with a 6 row Love Bite Lace pattern (reminiscent of vampire fangs!), is perfect for beginning lace knitters. It's solid enough to stylishly hide the evidence, but open enough to let in a passing breeze. Problem solved!*

## About this Project

**Skill Level:** Intermediate

**Finished Size:** Shown approximately 6" by 44" (15 x 112cm) after blocking; approximately 5" by 36" (13 x 91cm) before blocking

**Project Gauge:** 24 stitches and 30 rows = 4" (10cm) in stockinette stitch

*Note*: Gauge is not critical to this project but will impact the finished size and the amount of yarn used.

## Shopping List

Rowan Classic Yarns *Siena 4 Ply* (100% mercerized cotton; 153 yards/140m); 2 skeins White #651

Size US 6 (4mm) needles

Tapestry needle

## Stitch Guide

*Love Bite Lace*
Row 1: K3, *yo, ssk, k4, k2tog, yo, k1; repeat from * to last two stitches, k2.
Row 2: K3, p1, k6, p3, k6, p3, k6, p1, k3.
Row 3: K4, *yo, ssk, k2, k2tog, yo, k3; repeat from * to last stitch, k1.
Row 4: K3, p2, k4, p5, k4, p5, k4, p2, k3.
Row 5: K5, *yo, ssk, k2tog, yo, k5; repeat from * to end.
Row 6: K3, p3, k2, p7, k2, p7, k2, p3, k3.
Repeat row 1-6.

## Instructions

CO 2.

*Charted instructions*
Work Chart A. Repeat rows 37-42 twenty-eight times. (210 rows worked). Work Chart B. BO remaining stitches.

*Written instructions*
Row 1(RS): Knit.
Row 2 (WS): Knit.
Row 3: K1f&b twice. (4 stitches)
Row 4: Knit.
Row 5: K1f&b, knit to last stitch, k1f&b. (6 stitches)
Row 6: Knit.
Row 7-10: Repeat row 5 and 6 two times. (10 stitches)
Row 11: K1f&b, k2, yo, ssk, k2tog, yo, k2, k1f&b. (12 stitches)
Row 12: K3, p2, k2, p2, k3.
Row 13: K1f&b, k1, yo, ssk, k4, k2tog, yo, k1, k1f&b. (14 stitches)
Row 14: K3, p1, k6, p1, k3.
Row 15: K1f&b, k3, yo, ssk, k2, k2tog, yo, k3, k1f&b. (16 stitches)
Row 16: K3, p3, k4, p3, k3.

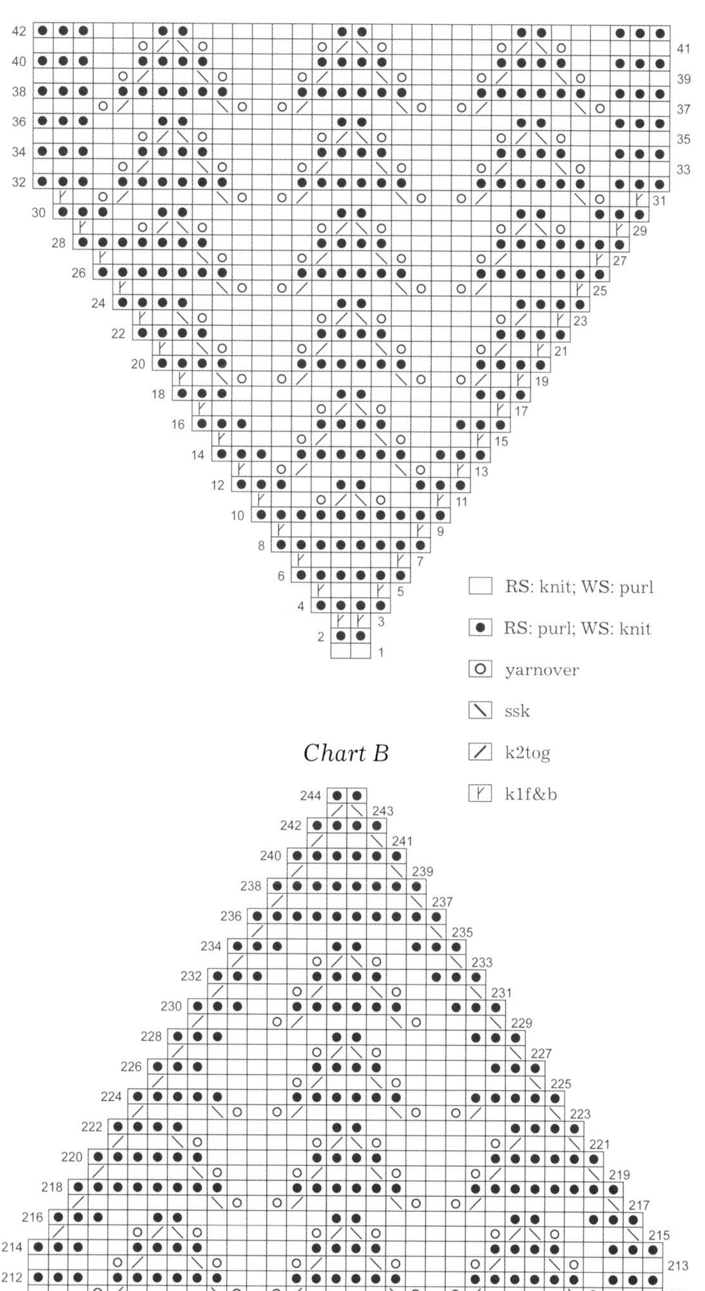


Row 17: K1f&b, k5, yo, ssk, k2tog, yo, k5, k1f&b. (18 stitches)
Row 18: K3, p5, k2, p5, k3.
Row 19: K1f&b, k1, k2tog, yo, k1, yo, ssk, k4, k2tog, yo, k1, yo, ssk, k1, k1f&b. (20 stitches)
Row 20: K4, p3, k6, p3, k4.
Row 21: K1f&b, k1, k2tog, yo, k3, yo, ssk, k2, k2tog, yo, k3, yo, ssk, k1, k1f&b. (22 stitches)
Row 22: K4, p5, k4, p5, k4.
Row 23: K1f&b, k1, k2tog, yo, k5, yo, ssk, k2tog, yo, k5, yo, ssk, k1, k1f&b. (24 stitches)
Row 24: K4, p7, k2, p7, k4.
Row 25: K1f&b, k4, k2tog, yo, k1, yo, ssk, k4, k2tog, yo, k1, yo, ssk, k4, k1f&b. (26 stitches)
Row 26: K7, p3, k6, p3, k7.
Row 27: K1f&b, k4, k2tog, yo, k3, yo, ssk, k2, k2tog, yo, k3, yo, ssk, k4, k1f&b. (28 stitches)
Row 28: K7, p5, k4, p5, k7.
Row 29: K1f&b, k2, yo, ssk, k2tog, yo, k5, yo, ssk, k2tog, yo, k5, yo, ssk, k2tog, yo, k2, k1f&b. (30 stitches)
Row 30: K3, p2, k2, p7, k2, p7, k2, p2, k3.
Row 31: K1f&b, k1, *yo, ssk, k4, k2tog, yo, k1; repeat from * to last stitch, k1f&b. (32 stitches)
Row 32: K3, p1, k6, p3, k6, p3, k6, p1, k3.
Row 33: K4, *yo, ssk, k2, k2tog, yo, k3; repeat from * to last stitch, k1.
Row 34: K3, p2, k4, p5, k4, p5, k4, p2, k3.
Row 35: K5, *yo, ssk, k2tog, yo, k5; repeat from * to end.
Row 36: K3, p3, k2, p7, k2, p7, k2, p3, k3.
Row 37-210: Work 29 repeats of *Love Bite Lace.*
Row 211: K3, *yo, ssk, k4, k2tog, yo, k1; repeat from * to last two stitches, k2. (32 stitches)
Row 212: K3, p1, k6, p3, k6, p3, k6, p1, k3.
Row 213: K4, *yo, ssk, k2, k2tog, yo, k3; repeat from * to last stitch, k1. (32 stitches)
Row 214: K3, p2, k4, p5, k4, p5, k4, p2, k3.
Row 215: Ssk, k3, *yo, ssk, k2tog, yo, k5, repeat from * to last 5 stitches, k3, k2tog. (30 stitches)
Row 216: K3, p2, k2, p7, k2, p7, k2, p2, k3.
Row 217: Ssk, k6, k2tog, yo, k1, yo, ssk, k4, k2tog, yo, k1, yo, ssk, k6, k2tog. (28 stitches)
Row 218: K8, p3, k6, p3, k8.

Row 219: Ssk, k4, k2tog, yo, k3, yo, ssk, k2, k2tog, yo, k3, yo, ssk, k4, k2tog. (26 stitches)
Row 220: K6, p5, k4, p5, k6.
Row 221: Ssk, k2, k2tog, yo, k5, yo, ssk, k2tog, yo, k5, yo, ssk, k2, k2tog. (24 stitches)
Row 222: K4, p7, k2, p7, k4.
Row 223: Ssk, k3, k2tog, yo, k1, yo, ssk, k4, k2tog, yo, k1, yo, ssk, k3, k2tog. (22 stitches)
Row 224: K5, p3, k6, p3, k5.
Row 225: Ssk, k6, yo, ssk, k2, k2tog, yo, k6, k2tog. (20 stitches)
Row 226: K3, p5, k4, p5, k3.
Row 227: Ssk, k6, yo, ssk, k2tog, yo, k6, k2tog. (18 stitches)
Row 228: K3, p5, k2, p5, k3.
Row 229: Ssk, k3, yo, ssk, k4, k2tog, yo, k3, k2tog. (16 stitches)
Row 230: K3, p2, k6, p2, k3.
Row 231: Ssk, k3, yo, ssk, k2, k2tog, yo, k3, k2tog. (14 stitches)
Row 232: K3, p2, k4, p2, k3.
Row 233: Ssk, k3, yo, ssk, k2tog, yo, k3, k2tog. (12 stitches)
Row 234: K3, p2, k2, p2, k3.
Row 235: Ssk, k to last 2 stitches, k2tog. (10 stitches)
Row 236: Knit.
Row 237-244: Repeat row 235 and 236 four times. (2 stitches)

BO remaining stitches.

## Finishing

Weave in ends. Soak scarf in cool water and roll in a towel to absorb most of the water. Do not wring. Pin out on a blocking board or other padded surface to open up the lace pattern. Allow to dry completely.

## Tips

- For charted knitting, odd-numbered rows (RS) are always worked right to left and even-numbered rows (WS) are worked left to right. This project is completely symmetrical, so you can work any row in either direction and it won't matter.
- You can make this scarf any length by simply adding more repeats of the 6 row *Love Bite Lace* pattern before beginning the decrease section.
- This yarn is machine washable, but don't toss it in the dryer. Always lay it flat and block it, then let it dry completely.
- Mercerized cotton yarns tend to have a tight twist that can sometimes tangle back on itself after a few rows. Just move the knitting to a safe spot on the needles (point protectors, too, for the faint of heart), grab the yarn right near the ball and let the work hang free while it untwists itself.
- Place a "lifeline" after every repeat or two to give yourself a place to rip back easily if you lose your spot or drop a stitch and can't get it back. If you choose to ignore this advice ... well, I told you so!
- No matter how easy the lace pattern, it's best not to stop in the middle of a row. Let the phone ring— it's probably one of those pesky pre-recorded telemarketers anyway.

# Magnolia Wristlets

New Orleans, Louisiana

*It is darn hot and muggy during the summer in New Orleans, and if we're being honest, spring, fall and sometimes even the winter can be more than a bit on the humid side. Locals combat the high humidity by cranking up the air conditioning. Public buildings are often kept so frigid as to resemble nothing as much as a meat locker. So despite the fact that it may be 100 degrees outside with the heat index, New Orleans' ladies find themselves needing a little something fluffy to protect from indoor chills at work.*

***Garden District Needlework's Julia Houston** to the rescue! These charming silk mohair wristlets keep cold air off tender hands and wrists while weighing almost nothing and leaving the fingers free to fly along the keyboard. Go full-on feminine with lace and floral trim or be a bit more conservative with a plain or button edging.*

## About this Project

**Skill Level:** Easy

**Finished Size:** Approximately 7" (18cm) in circumference by 9" (23cm) long including ruffle

**Project Gauge:** 22 stitches and 28 rows = 4" (10cm) on larger needles in stockinette stitch with one strand each of *Wool Cotton* and *Kidsilk Haze* held together

## Shopping List

Rowan *Wool Cotton* (50% merino wool, 50% cotton, 123 yards/113m); 1 skein Elf #946, 1 skein Antique #900

Rowan *Kidsilk Haze* (70% super kid mohair, 30% silk, 229 yards/210m); 1 skein Jelly #597

Size US 2 (2.75mm) needles

Size US 6 (4mm) needles

Tapestry needle

Length of worsted or aran weight yellow yarn (optional)

Buttons, beads or fabric flowers to trim top edge (optional)

## Instructions

With larger needles and one strand each of *Wool Cotton* Antique #900 and *Kidsilk Haze* held together, CO 40 stitches.
Row 1 (RS): Knit.
Row 2 (WS): Purl.
Row 3 and 5: *K1, p1; repeat from * until end.
Row 4 and 6: *P1, k1; repeat from * until end.
Cut *Wool Cotton* Antique, leaving 6" (15cm) tail.
Join *Wool Cotton* Elf.
Row 7-14: With one strand each of *Wool Cotton* Elf #946 and *Kidsilk Haze* held together, work 8 rows of stockinette stitch.
*Thumb opening*
*Right hand only*
Row 15: K10, BO 6, k24.
Row 16: P24, CO 6, p10.
*Left hand only*
Row 15: K24, BO 6, k10.
Row 16: P10, CO 6, p24.
*Both hands*
Continue in stockinette stitch until piece measures 6" (15cm) from cast on edge.
*Begin decreases*
Continuing in stockinette stitch, BO 2 stitches at the beginning of every row until 8 stitches remain. BO remaining stitches.
*Knitted ruffle trim*
With one strand of *Kidsilk Haze* only and smaller needles, pick up and knit 40 stitches around the curved lower edge of the wristlet.
Row 1 (WS): K1f&b into each stitch. (80 stitches)
Row 2: K1f&b into each stitch. (160 stitches)
BO all stitches.

*Garden District Needlework* is the Southeast's largest yarn and needlework shop. Located on Magazine Street in the historic Garden District, it's a must-see for knitters and crocheters visiting the Big Easy. Find them online at GardenDistrictNeedlework.biz.

## Finishing

With tapestry needle and *Wool Cotton* Elf, sew side seam of wristlet from CO edge to where decreases begin. Weave in ends.

Decorate the seed stitch area across the knuckles with six French knots in the yellow yarn (yarn used in picture is Rowan *Summer Cotton*). Alternately, the *Wool Cotton* Elf may be used exclusively and the decorations can be buttons or beads.

## Celebrations New Orleans Style

A historic city full of architectural gems and tantalizing Cajun cuisine, New Orleans has figured out how to turn the most mundane holidays into unforgettable events. In addition to the infamous New Orleans Mardi Gras— two weeks of debauched revelry leading up to Ash Wednesday— this city celebrates in style year round.

More family-friendly than Mardi Gras, the "wearin' of the green" for St. Patrick's Day is celebrated in the Crescent City by parades with floats (of course!) and lots of "throws." In addition to traditional Mardi Gras style beads and throws in green and gold, float riders toss anything arguably Irish, from cabbages and potatoes to boxes of Lucky Charms® cereal and bars of Irish Spring® soap!

Valentine's Day is wedding day in nearby Gretna, named for Gretna Green in Scotland. Gretna Green was *the* place for runaway couples in Victorian England to elope for quickie weddings. In Louisiana's Gretna, couples wed at the historic blacksmith shop to the music of bagpipes. The wedding license is even sealed on the anvil, a tradition in Gretna Green.

Late April-early May brings hundreds of thousands of music fans to the renowned New Orleans Jazz Festival. Ten days and twelve stages featuring the best musicians in the world, the festival also hosts stunning arts and crafts on the weekends. And did someone mention Cajun food? There's more catfish, crawfish, soft shell crab, gator, and red beans than you can shake a po'boy sandwich at. Our advice? Wear stretchy pants.

# Bananas Foster Bread Pudding

*Bananas Foster is a classic New Orleans dessert made with flambéed bananas, brown sugar and bourbon over vanilla ice cream. This dessert takes it up a notch with hot bread pudding studded with ripe bananas, topped with warm, bubbly brown sugar pecan bourbon sauce and then double-topped with chilled vanilla custard sauce. You're welcome!*

## Directions

Preheat oven to 325 degrees. Butter an 8"x8" baking dish. Tear bread into a bowl and set aside.

In a large bowl, combine sweetened condensed milk and eggs; blend well. Add sliced bananas, orange juice, hot water, melted butter, cinnamon, and vanilla. Stir in bread chunks, moistening completely. Let sit 10 minutes or until liquid is mostly soaked up. Turn into prepared baking dish. Bake about 1 hour or until a knife inserted in center comes out clean. Cool slightly and serve warm with Pecan Fosters Sauce and Vanilla Custard Cream Sauce. If you really want to live decadently, top the pudding and sauces with a big dollop of fresh sweetened whipped cream. Cover and refrigerate leftovers, if you have any. The pudding warmed without the sauce makes a great breakfast the next day.

*Pecan Foster Sauce*
Melt butter. Remove from heat. Add brown sugar and mix to form a smooth paste. Slowly stir in rum or whiskey until sauce is smooth. Warm over very low heat. Stir in pecans and serve warm over the bread pudding.

*Vanilla Custard Cream Sauce*
Mix flour with 3 tablespoons of the half-and-half to form a smooth paste. Slowly stir in the remaining half-and-half, beating to keep lumps from forming. Add remaining ingredients except for the vanilla extract. Transfer to small saucepan and bring to a boil over medium heat, stirring frequently to prevent lumps from forming. Remove from heat. Add vanilla. Serve warm over bread pudding.

Serves 6-8.

### Shopping List

*Bread Pudding*

4 cups torn French bread
1 can (14oz) sweetened condensed milk
3 large eggs
2 cups sliced fresh bananas
1/2 cup orange juice
1 1/4 cups hot water
4 Tbl butter, melted
1 tsp pure vanilla extract
1 tsp cinnamon

*Pecan Foster Sauce*

4 Tbl butter
1 cup dark brown sugar, packed
2 oz dark rum or whiskey
1 cup chopped pecans

*Vanilla Custard Sauce*

2 cups half-and-half
1 egg, beaten
1/2 cup sugar
3 Tbl flour
1 Tbl pure vanilla extract

Leaving Cocoa Beach, Florida for college in Columbus, Mississippi was a bracing bit of culture shock. First, my Mom never fried *anything*. I had no idea what okra was, couldn't figure out how you'd chicken-fry a steak, and the sight of Red Velvet Cake was terrifying. It didn't take me long to dive into the menu though, and the fabled Freshman 15 swelled to something more like a Freshman 25. The next surprise was Mississippi's sense of time. An "old" house in Cocoa Beach was 20 years old! I swooned over the beautiful antebellum architecture and deep sense of history in my new home. It was the beginning of my love affair with the Deep South.

Mississippi's homes and gardens capture my imagination more than any other Southern state. There's no better place to experience the grand architecture of the Civil War era than in Natchez, the oldest city on the Mississippi River. Cotton was king in Natchez, and wealthy plantation owners didn't pinch pennies when it came to building extravagant homes. About a dozen of those estates are open to the public year-round, and several more can be toured during Pilgrimage, a five-week event held every spring and fall. The home on the cover of *Deep South Knitting* is Stanton Hall, site of the Pilgrimage Garden Club. Other homes on the don't-miss list are Rosalie, which served as Union headquarters during the Civil War, and the stunning but unfinished Longwood, an onion-domed octagon of a mansion that fans of the True Blood® television series will recognize as the Vampire King of Mississippi's home.

Natchez sits on the highest point of the river. The 200 foot bluffs provide the perfect vantage point to watch calliope-playing paddle-wheelers cruise the Mighty Mississippi, while the Louisiana lowlands shimmer in the distance. The music floating over the water creates a magical illusion of the easy pace of times long past.

Natchez isn't all Civil War history. If you like the blues and love biscuits (who doesn't?), you have to check out Biscuits & Blues, America's #1 rated blues club. Whether you get the fried catfish, smoked ribs or a po'boy sandwich, your tummy and ears will both be thanking you.

# Darlin' Tea Cozy

Natchez, Mississippi

*If you want a real taste of the antebellum South, the Spring or Fall Pilgrimage in Natchez, Mississippi is guaranteed to do the trick. For a few weeks each year, many of the city's spectacularly preserved mansions open their doors and grounds to visitors. Strolling the gardens where the creamy magnolia blossoms perch among glossy green and copper leaves, you can't help but drift off to a time when belles in hoop skirts fluttered their eyelashes while they sipped tea, and refined, lanky men in white linen suits vied for their attention.*

*This tea cozy was inspired by the genteel pace and lavish blossoms of Mississippi. And at the risk of being thought too flashy to be truly ladylike, there's just a little bit of shine, courtesy of a few golden glass beads. Not enough to be trashy, mind you. Just a bit of girly to keep your tea pot warm while you nibble daintily on a slice of Red Velvet Cake.*

## About this Project

**Skill Level:** Intermediate

**Finished Size:** Approximately 10" (25cm) high by 12" (30cm) wide and 24" (60cm) circumference at bottom after felting; 15" (38cm) wide by 15" (38cm) high and 30" (75cm) circumference at bottom before felting

**Project Gauge:** 13.5 stitches and 17 rows = approximately 4" (10cm) in stockinette stitch with two strands of yarn held together on size US 11 (8mm) needles before felting

## Shopping List

Cascade *220 Wool* (100% Peruvian highland wool, 220 yards/200m); 2 skeins Natural #8010, 1 skein White #8505 for blossoms, half skein Forest Green #8267, half skein Shamrock #9486, half skein Japanese Maple #2435, small amount Goldenrod #7827 for flower centers and needle-felted trim

Size US 7 (4.5mm) needles

Size US 9 (5.5mm) needles

Size US 11 (8mm) double pointed needles

Size US 11 (8mm) 20-24" (50-60cm) circular needle

Stitch markers

Tapestry needle

Needle-felting needles

Dressmaker's removable marking pencil

Approximately 72 dark yellow glass size 6/0 beads

Sewing needle

Embroidery floss in matching and complementary shades (see *Tips*)

## Stitch Guide

*Wrap & turn (wr&t)*
All worked on RS: Bring yarn to front of needle, as if to purl. Slip one stitch from left hand needle to right hand needle, as if to purl. Bring yarn to back. Slip stitch back to right hand needle. Turn work.

## Instructions

*Tea cozy base*
With US 11 (8mm) circular needle and <u>two</u> strands of Natural held together, CO 100 stitches. Place marker and join for working in the round, being careful not to twist stitches.
Row 1: K50, place marker, k50. Slip marker.
Row 2-30: Knit, slipping markers.
Row 31: *Ssk, knit to two stitches before marker, k2tog, slip marker, repeat from * to end. (96 stitches)
Row 32: Knit.
Row 33-60: Repeat rows 31-32 fourteen times. (40 stitches)
Row 61-66: Repeat row 31 six times. (16 stitches)
Move 8 stitches to each of two double pointed needles. Using three-needle bind off, BO the remaining stitches.

*Magnolia blossoms (make 4)*
*Inside petals (make 1 for each magnolia blossom, 4 total)*
With US 7 (4.5mm) needles and <u>one</u> strand of White, using knitted cast on, CO 4 stitches.
Row 1: K1f&b, k2, wr&t. (5 stitches)
Row 2: P4.
Row 3-6: Repeat rows 1-2 twice. (7 stitches)
Row 7: Knit all 7 stitches, picking up wraps.
Row 8: Purl.
Row 9: K2tog, k3, wr&t. (6 stitches)
Row 10: Purl.
Row 11-14: Repeat rows 9-10 twice, picking up wraps as they present themselves. (4 stitches)
Row 15: K2tog twice. (2 stitches)
Row 16: Purl.

Row 17: Turn. Using knitted cast on, CO 2 stitches. (4 stitches)
Row 18-34: Repeat rows 1-17.
Row 35-49: Repeat rows 1-15.
Row 50: P2tog. Cut yarn, leaving 8" tail. Pull tail through remaining loop.

*Outside petals (make 2 sets for each blossom, 8 total)*
With US 7 (4.5mm) needles and one strand of White, CO 7 stitches.
Row 1: K1f&b, k5, wr&t. (8 stitches)
Row 2: Purl.
Row 3-10: Repeat rows 1-2 four times. (12 stitches)
Row 11: Knit, picking up wraps.
Row 12: Purl.
Row 13: Knit.
Row 14: Purl.
Row 15: K2tog, k6, wr&t. (11 stitches)
Row 16: Purl.
Row 17-24: Repeat rows 15-16 four times. (7 stitches)
Row 25: K2tog three times, k1. (4 stitches)
Row 26: P2tog twice. (2 stitches)
Row 27: K2.
Row 28: P2. Turn and using knitted cast on, CO 5 stitches. (7 stitches)
Row 29-56: Repeat rows 1-28.
Row 57-82: Repeat rows 1-26.
Row 83: K2tog. Cut yarn, leaving 8" tail. Pull tail through remaining loop.

*Flower center (make 4)*
With US 7 (4.5mm) needles and one strand of Goldenrod, CO 4 stitches.
Row 1: K1f&b, knit to last stitch, k1f&b. (6 stitches)
Row 2 and all even numbered rows: Purl.
Row 3: K1f&b, knit to last stitch, k1f&b. (8 stitches)
Row 5: Knit.
Row 7: K2tog, knit to last 2 stitches, k2tog. (6 stitches)
Row 9: K2tog, knit to last 2 stitches, k2tog. (4 stitches)
Row 11: Slip three stitches knitwise one at a time. K1. Pass three slip stitches one at a time over knitted stitch. Cut yarn, leaving 8" tail. Draw tail through remaining stitch.
Thread tail through a tapestry needle. Draw yarn in and out through outside edge with a running stitch. Draw up, with smooth stockinette side to the outside, creating a ball shape. Tie off.

*Leaves*
The leaves are cut from knitted sheets of felt. For each of the three colors, use half a skein (approximately 110 yards). For each color, with US 9 (5.5mm) needles and one strand, CO 50 stitches. Knit until just enough left to bind off. BO all stitches.

## Finishing

Join each string of three flower petals into a ring by threading the tail through a tapestry needle and basting close to the inner edge of the three petals and pulling the yarn to create a closed ring. Knot and tie closed. Layer one ring of the larger outside petals on the bottom, with the petals at 10, 2, and 6 o'clock. Center a second ring of the larger outside petals on top of the first ring, with the petals at 12, 4, and 8 o'clock. Center a ring of the smaller inside petals on top of the two rings with the petals at 10, 2, and 6 o'clock. Thread a tapestry needle with a short length of the yarn. Stitch through all three layers of petals in a short running stitch all around the center ring, making sure to stitch at least twice through each petal. Tie off.

Tightly felt the tea cozy base, blossoms and centers. Felt the sheets for the leaves separately from the base, blossoms and centers to avoid dark felt from accumulating on the lighter base. Do not spin dry. For the blossoms, while still wet, shape petals into a cupped shape, smoothing outside edges and stretching into shape where needed. Place the wet flower in a small round bowl or large cup to maintain shape and allow to dry. For tea cozy base, stretch and smooth as needed and prop open over a tall narrow box to dry. For blossom centers, stretch and smooth into a round ball and allow to dry. For leaf sheets, stretch and smooth flat and allow to dry. After drying, clip any felted loose ends from the inside of the cozy base.

When all pieces are fully dry, attach blossom center to blossom with three strands of embroidery floss, stitching all the way through the flower and the center and adding a bead on top before stitching back down toward bottom. The blossoms shown in the photo have each been embellished with 12 size 6/0 glass beads. You can omit the beads or use more or less depending on your preference.

Cut leaf shapes approximately 2¼" (5cm) wide and 4" (10cm) high. The number of leaves you get will depend on how tightly you felted. We were able to cut 8 Japanese Maple, 8 Shamrock, and 17 Forest Green leaves from our felt sheets. You may get more or less. Using the photo as a guide, with three strands of embroidery floss in a complementary shade slightly lighter than the color of the leaf (see *Tips*), embroider leaves using a running stitch to create the veins. Apply leaves to the tea cozy, attaching with blanket stitch embroidery and using three strands of embroidery floss that matches the leaf color, overlapping leaves. Attach blossoms on top of the leaves with three strands of off-white embroidery floss, stitching close to the base of the petals.

No flower is more associated with the South than creamy white magnolias. Just before blooming, they draw up their glossy leaves to show off their coppery velvet undersides.

Using a dressmaker's removable marking pencil, sketch your choice of text for the open areas of both sides of the tea cozy. Using one strand of Shamrock #9486, needle-felt your text. Do the same for the scroll designs, using the Goldenrod #7827 yarn. Set the needle-felting with a hot iron and a damp cloth. With three strands of yellow embroidery floss, stitch beads as desired to the text and scrolls.

## Tips

- In a hurry? If you have a knitting machine, you can knit the stockinette sheets for the leaves. Even more of a hurry? You can hand knit the flowers and buy commercial felt for the rest of the projects, cutting two pieces for the tea cozy base and stitching them together with blanket stitch and 6 strands of embroidery floss in gold or green. We won't tell a soul, promise.
- Different colors of yarn can felt differently, even in the same brand and weight. For this project, it won't matter. If some of your leaves are a bit thicker than others, it's OK. Just keep an eye on all the pieces during felting and remove any pieces that complete the felting process ahead of the others.
- If you decide to substitute yarns for this project, make sure you test your white yarn to make sure it will felt. Depending on the manufacturer's process, the white may have lost all its scales in the bleaching process and the yarn won't felt.
- You can choose more or less contrast with your embroidery. We used the following shades of DMC embroidery floss: one skein 500, 780, 972, 988 and 3858, and two skeins of 986.
- Basic felting instructions are included in the pattern for the Mardi Gras Party Bangles.
- If you've never needle-felted, I have a free online class on PlanetPurl.com.

# Bayou Boa

Biloxi, Mississippi

*Throughout the South, from the yards of humble low-country cottages, to the grounds of lavish antebellum mansions, to the swampy bayous of Biloxi and the Gulf Coast, everywhere you look are oak trees dressed up for a garden party with their streamers of curly Spanish moss. Stirring gently in a welcome breeze, the moss shifts from green to silvery gray and back again. The tendrils catch the summer rain, adding a magical little shimmer to the surface.*

*This lightweight boa is as gossamer as a spider web and will flutter gracefully in the slightest breeze. A touch of silk in the yarn gives the barest shimmer, reminiscent of the tiny diamond drops of rain captured by the moss and glistening in the summer sun. Wear it and create your own bit of a stir.*

## About this Project

**Skill Level:** Easy

**Finished Size:** Approximately 96" (2.4m) long by 7" (18cm) wide

**Project Gauge:** 9 foundation chain stitches = 4" (10cm). Work very loosely in order to achieve the airiness of this design.

## Shopping List

Rowan *Kidsilk Haze* (70% super kid mohair, 30% silk, 229 yards/210m); 9 skeins each Meadow #581 and Pearl #590

Size US N-15 (9mm) crochet hook

Tapestry needle

## Stitch Guide

*Spanish Lace Edging (8 stitch repeat)*
Round 1: Ch 1, sc in each trc around. Join with a slip stitch in first sc to complete the round.
Round 2: *Sc, sk 3 sc, [trc, ch 1] 5 times in next sc, trc once more in same sc, ch4, sk 3 sc; repeat from * to end.

## Instructions

With one strand of each color held together, chain 181. The chain should measure approximately 80" (2m). See *Tips* section below. You will now be working up one side and down the other side of the chain.
Round 1: Skip one ch, then 1 sc in each chain space down the first side of the chain, 7 sc in the last chain. Rotate work 180 degrees and work 1 sc in other side of each chain, 6 additional sc in end chain, join with a slip stitch in first sc to complete the round. (370 sc)
Round 2: Ch 2. Work 2 hdc in each sc. Slip stitch to complete the round. (740 hdc)
Round 3: Ch 3. Work 2 dc in each hdc. Slip stitch to complete the round. (1480 dc)
Round 4: Ch 4. Work 2 trc in each dc. Slip stitch to complete the round. (2960 trc)
*Edging*
Work both rounds of *Spanish Lace Edging*, joining with a slip stitch to complete each round. Fasten off.

## Finishing

Weave in all ends. Fluff, fluff, fluff.

## Tips

- You cannot work too loosely on this project. If your chain is shorter than 80" (2m) you can just keep chaining until you reach the desired length, but it will significantly increase the amount of yarn needed and will create a denser boa. It's better to rip back the chain and start over here than after you're done!
- If you occasionally make one stitch where two stitches are called for, just keep working. Trust me, it won't show. A tiny shift in stitch count is really unimportant until you're ready to add the edging. During the single crochet round (round 1) of the *Spanish Lace Edging*, make sure your stitch count is evenly divisible by 8, adding a few single crochet increases if necessary.

Spanish moss makes its home in Southern live oaks and bald cypress. It loves high humidity, which might account for the curls? The tendrils can grow to 20 feet long, creating lovely, silvery drapes.

## Mississippi Blues

Music has always been a huge part of Mississippi's heritage. You can follow the Mississippi Blues Trail (msbluestrail.org) through every corner of the state and visit the birthplaces of dozens of the world's greatest blues musicians and even have a drink in some of the juke joints where they played.

*B.B. King*, Berclair - Birthplace of the King of the Blues.

*John Lee Hooker*, Vance - One of the most famous bluesmen of all time, Hooker was born in the Delta where he learned to play guitar. He was inducted into both the Blues and the Rock & Roll Halls of Fame.

*Muddy Waters*, Clarksdale - Waters moved to Clarksdale while young. Later, he ran a juke joint out of his cabin where he entertained field hands on the Stovall plantation where he lived. Billy Gibbons (ZZ Top) had guitars made from planks of the cabin which were used for fundraising for the Delta Blues Museum.

*Robert Johnson*, Greenwood - Johnson was born and was buried in the Delta. His gravesite is in Greenwood, where he was rumored to have been poisoned by a jealous husband.

*Bo Diddley*, McComb - The father of rock and roll was born outside McComb in 1928.

*Elvis Presley*, Tupelo - The King grew up on gospel and blues in Tupelo, then blended it with country and pop and created a sound that changed music forever.

# Red Velvet Cake

*This cake, responsible for 15 pounds gained during my freshman year at Mississippi University for Women, almost defies description— but we'll try. Three moist layers of buttermilk devil's food cake, the color of deep red velvet, are covered with the lightest, fluffiest boiled milk frosting, then studded with walnuts and dusted with coconut. Bake it and believe.*

## Directions

Preheat oven to 350 degrees. Grease and flour three 8" round cake pans.

*Cake*
Mix together all dry ingredients until cocoa is evenly dispersed and flour is evenly darkened. Beat together eggs and oil until well mixed and slightly frothy. Add egg mixture, buttermilk, coloring and vanilla to the dry ingredients. Mix well until smooth. Take care not to spatter the cake batter while stirring as the food coloring will stain. Pour batter into three greased and floured 8" cake pans. The pans may look like there is not enough batter, but this cake batter really rises. You may substitute two 9" round pans, but you will lose an extra layer of frosting and that's just too sad for me to contemplate. Bake for 30 minutes (35 minutes if using two 9" pans) or until toothpick inserted at center comes out clean. Cool on racks. Allow to cool completely before assembling.

*Milk frosting*
Combine flour with 2 tablespoons of the milk and stir until smooth. Stir in rest of the milk slowly, stirring constantly to prevent lumps. Cook over low heat, stirring constantly. Do not boil. Cook over low heat until thick, almost to the consistency of cake batter. Set aside and allow to cool completely. Stir occasionally while cooling to prevent lumps from forming. The milk/flour mixture will continue to thicken as it cools. After milk/flour mixture is completely cool, cut slightly softened butter into 1" cubes and cream with sugar using electric mixer until light and fluffy and no longer gritty. Add vanilla and cooled milk/flour mixture. Don't get impatient and add the flour mixture before it is completely cooled or the frosting will be ruined. Beat at high speed until icing becomes stiff, fluffy and smooth. Refrigerate, covered until ready to use.

*Cake assembly*
When the cake is completely cool, ice two of three layers with the milk frosting. On one layer, press in cup of chopped walnuts. Place second layer on top of layer with walnuts. On the second layer, sprinkle half the coconut. Top with third layer. Frost sides and top. Press remaining chopped walnuts into sides of cake. Sprinkle remaining coconut on top. Keep covered in refrigerator.

## Shopping List

*For the Cake*

2 1/2 cups all purpose flour
1 1/2 cups sugar
2 eggs
2 Tbl cocoa
2 oz red food coloring
1 tsp salt
1 tsp pure vanilla extract
1 cup buttermilk
1 2/3 cups vegetable oil
1 tsp baking soda
1 Tbl vinegar

*Milk Frosting*

2 cups milk
2 1/2 cups granulated sugar
1/2 cup flour
1 1/2 cups slightly softened unsalted butter
2 tsp pure vanilla extract

*Cake Assembly*

1 1/2 cups chopped walnuts
1 1/2 cups sweetened flaked coconut

When I was in college in Mississippi, my boyfriend at the time took me, via motorcycle, to visit his sister in Atlanta. Somewhere in the middle of Alabama, late at night, the motorcycle broke down. It was freezing cold out. I put on every piece of clothing I packed, but still shivered. A state trooper saw us and came to help. He stopped a passing pickup truck and they lifted the bike into the bed. They took us to the closest town, and woke up a local mechanic, who came out to fix the bike. When I think of Alabama I remember that small-town, no-such-thing-as-a-stranger attitude that epitomizes the best of Southern traditions.

Birmingham and Mobile are the state's largest cities, but both still have that friendly small-town feel where strangers are welcomed with a smile and a "Good morning." These cities offer a wealth of history, many gorgeous gardens, and great regional cooking.

Birmingham was central to the Civil Right movement, and the area is full of museums and historical sites that document the events of that era. Baseball fans will enjoy the Museum of Negro League and Southern League Baseball History. It's next to Rickwood Field, the world's oldest ballpark, now restored to its original appearance. Quilters and lovers of textile arts should not miss 'That's Sew Gee's Bend.' You can learn about the Gee's Bend story— a collective of freed slaves (and now their descendants) who create stunning graphic quilts that are one-of-a-kind marvels of modern art— and hear the women sing historic gospel songs as they quilt.

Mobile is Alabama's oldest city, and it's a treasure trove for lovers of gardens and architecture. The Bellingrath Gardens and Home are a must-see, and just one of many historic homes open to visitors. Christmas addicts (like me!) should make a beeline for Christmas Town, over 35,000 square feet of holiday decor and collectibles by Robert Moore & Co. And the Southern Market, built in 1857, houses the Museum of Mobile, sure to delight any history buff.

Head to Alabama— your neighbors and friends are waiting to meet you!

# Alabama

# Camellia Baby Set

Birmingham, Alabama

In the Southern states, the dead of winter is interrupted by the blooming of camellias, resplendent in creamy white and shades of pink, emerging from the shelter of their glossy leaves. They hold a special place for Alabamans, who have shown their exquisite taste by selecting it as their state flower. The Camellia Garden at the Birmingham Botanical Gardens is one of the best places to enjoy this Southern beauty.

This sweet baby bunting and bonnet set celebrates both the camellia and the birth of a lucky baby girl. Knit in a soft blend of merino, cashmere and silk, its flower petal trim and soft colors evoke Alabama's favorite flower. The snaps up the front allow easy in-and-out and the bottom can be left unsnapped to strap the little angel into a car seat. When the drawstring is pulled, the bottom of the bunting becomes a white camellia blossom. Minimal shaping and simple garter stitch put this project within the reach of an adventurous beginner.

## About this Project

**Skill Level:** Easy-mediate

**Finished Size:** 40" (102cm) in circumference at hem; 27½" (70cm) in circumference at chest when snapped; 23" (58cm) from shoulder to drawstring

**Project Gauge:** 20 stitches and 40 rows = 4" (10cm) in garter stitch

### Shopping List

Sublime *Baby Cashmere Merino Silk DK* (75% extra fine merino wool, 20% silk, 5% cashmere, 127 yards/116m); 7 skeins Waterlily #005 (MC), 5 skeins Mousse #121 (CC)

2 sets size US 6 (4mm) needles

Size US 6 (4mm) double pointed needles

Tapestry needle

24" (60cm) snap tape

## Instructions

### Bunting

*Front*
*Right front skirt*
*For Flower Petal hem, with MC, CO 4 stitches.
Row 1 (RS): Knit.
Row 2 (WS): K1, yo, k2, yo, k1. (6 stitches)
Row 3 and all RS rows: Knit.
Row 4: K1, yo, k4, yo, k1. (8 stitches)
Row 6: K1, yo, k6, yo, k1. (10 stitches)
Row 8, 10 & 12: K1, yo, k2tog, k4, ssk, yo, k1. (10 stitches)
Row 13: Knit.
Row 14: Knit.
Break yarn. Leave on RH needle.
Repeat from * for 4 more petals. Do not break yarn after last petal.
*Note:* For all petal trim on bunting and hat, before knitting across all the stitches to join the petals, make sure all the cast on tails and final row tails of each petal hang from the right edge of the petal when needle with petals is held in the left hand.
Row 15: Knit across all petals to join. (50 stitches)
Row 16-17: Knit.
Row 18: CO 1 stitch using knitted cast on to create side selvedge stitch. Knit to end. (51 stitches)
Row 19: Knit.
Row 20: P1, knit to last stitch, p1.
Row 21-26: Repeat rows 19-20 three times.
Row 27 (eyelet row): *K3, yo, k2tog; repeat from * to last stitch, k1. (51 stitches)
Row 28: P1, knit to last stitch, p1.
Row 29 (flange row): Using knitted cast on, CO 3, knit to end. (54 stitches)
Row 30: P1, knit to last stitch, p1.
Row 31: Knit.
Row 32: P1, knit to last stitch, p1.
Repeat rows 31-32 until piece measures 1" (2.5cm) from eyelet row, ending with a WS row.

*Decrease row (RS)*: Knit to last 3 stitches, k2tog, k1.
Repeat row 32. Continue working as in rows 31 and 32, repeating the *decrease row* on RS rows at 2, 3, 4, 5, 6, 7, 8, 8½, 9, 9½ , 10, 10½, 11, 11½, 12, 12½, and 13" (5, 8, 10, 13, 15, 18, 20, 22, 23, 24, 25, 27, 28, 29, 30, 32, and 33cm) from the
eyelet row. (36 stitches).
Work as in rows 31 and 32 until piece measures 15" (38cm) from eyelet row, ending with a WS row.

*Right front bodice*

*Note:* Use second pair of needles for petal trim of bodice.
*With CC, CO 4 stitches.
Row 1 (RS): Knit.
Row 2 (WS): K1, yo, k2, yo, k1. (6 stitches)
Row 3: Knit.
Row 4: K1, yo, k4, yo, k1. (8 stitches)
Row 5: Knit.
Row 6: K1, yo, k2tog, k2, ssk, yo, k1. (8 stitches)
Row 7-12: Repeat rows 5-6 three times.
Row 13-14: Knit.
Break yarn. Leave on RH needle.
Repeat from * for 3 more petals. Do not break yarn after last petal.
Row 15: Knit across all petals to join. (32 stitches)
Row 16: Knit. Break yarn.
Join CC to flange edge of right front skirt. K3. Hold bodice petal trim section in front of the skirt section. Join bodice trim to the skirt by knitting one stitch of the bodice from the front needle together with one stitch from the skirt section of the back needle. Join all bodice stitches. Knit remaining skirt stitch. (36 stitches).
Next row: With CC, p1, knit to last stitch, p1.
Continue working evenly with CC as in rows 31 and 32 of the skirt section until piece measures 20¾" (53cm) from eyelet row, ending with a WS row.

*Right front neck shaping*

Row 1 (RS): BO 7 stitches at neck edge, knit to end. (29 stitches)
Row 2 (WS): P1, knit to end.
Row 3: K2tog at neck edge, knit to end. (28 stitches)
Row 4: P1, knit to end.
Row 5-16: Repeat rows 3 and 4 six times. (22 stitches)
Row 17: Knit.
Row 18: P1, knit to end.
Row 19: Knit.
Row 20: P1, knit to end.
BO all stitches.

*Left front*

Repeat as for right front, decreasing along outside edge of skirt, and reversing neck and shoulder shaping as follows: Work until piece measures 20¾" (53cm) from eyelet row, ending with a WS row.

*Left front neck shaping*

Row 1 (RS): Knit.
Row 2 (WS): BO 7 stitches at neck edge, knit to last stitch, p1. (29 stitches)
Row 3: Knit.
Row 4: K2tog at neck edge, knit to last stitch, p1. (28 stitches)
Row 5-16: Repeat rows 3 and 4 six times. (22 stitches)
Row 17: Knit.
Row 18: Knit to last stitch, p1.
Row 19: Knit.
Row 20: Knit to last stitch, p1.
BO all stitches.

*Back*

*For Flower Petal hem, with MC, CO 4 stitches.
Row 1 (RS): Knit.
Row 2 (WS): K1, yo, k2, yo, k1. (6 stitches)
Row 3 and all RS rows: Knit.
Row 4: K1, yo, k4, yo, k1. (8 stitches)
Row 6: K1, yo, k6, yo, k1. (10 stitches)
Row 8, 10 & 12: K1, yo, k2tog, k4, ssk, yo, k1. (10 stitches)
Row 13-14: Knit.
Break yarn. Leave on RH needle.
Repeat from * for 9 more petals. Do not break yarn after last petal.
Row 15: Knit across all petals to join. (100 stitches)
Row 16: Knit.
Row 17: CO 1 stitch using knitted cast on to create side selvedge stitch. Knit to end. (101 stitches)
Row 18: CO 1 stitch using knitted cast on to create side selvedge stitch. Knit to last stitch, p1. (102 stitches)
Row 19: Knit.
Row 20: P1, knit to last stitch, p1.
Row 21-26: Repeat rows 19-20 three times.
Row 27 (eyelet row): K4, yo, k2tog, *k3, yo, k2tog; repeat from * to last stitch, k1. (102 stitches)
Row 28: P1, knit to last stitch, p1.
Row 29: Knit.
Row 30: P1, knit to last stitch, p1.
Repeat rows 29-30 until piece measures 1" (2.5cm) from eyelet row, ending with a WS row.

*Decrease row (RS)*: K1, ssk, knit to last 3 stitches, k2tog, k1.
Repeat row 30. Continue working as in row 29 and 30, repeating the *decrease row* on RS rows at 2, 3, 4, 5, 6, 7, 8, 9, 10, 11, 12, 12½, and 13" (5, 8, 10, 13, 15, 18, 20, 23, 25, 28, 30, 32 and 33cm) from the eyelet row. (74 stitches).
Work as in rows 29-30 until piece measures 15" (38cm) from eyelet row, ending with a WS row.

*Back bodice*

With second pair of needles, CC and following instructions for 8-stitch petals for the front bodice, make 9 petals. Do not break yarn after last petal.
Knit across all petals to join. (72 stitches). Knit 1 additional row and break yarn.
Join CC to right edge of skirt back. K1. Hold bodice section in front of the skirt section. Join bodice to the skirt by knitting one stitch of the bodice from the front needle together with one stitch of the skirt section from back needle. Join all bodice stitches. Knit remaining skirt stitch. (74 stitches).
Next row: With CC, p1, knit to last stitch, p1.
Continue working evenly with CC as in rows 29-30 of the back skirt instructions until piece measures 21½" (55cm) from eyelet row, ending with a WS row.

*Back neck shaping*

Row 1: K30, BO 14 stitches, k30. From this point, work shoulders separately.

*Left shoulder*

Row 1 (WS): P1, knit to end. (30 stitches)
Row 2 (RS): BO 4 stitches at neck edge, knit to end. (26 stitches)

Row 3: P1, knit to end.
Row 4: K2tog, knit to end. (25 stitches)
Row 5-10: Repeat rows 3-4 three times. (22 stitches)
Row 11: P1, knit to end.
BO remaining 22 stitches.

*Right shoulder*

Reattach yarn to neck edge of remaining side, preparing to work a WS row.
Row 1 (WS): BO 4 at neck edge, knit to last stitch, p1. (26 stitches)
Row 2 (RS): Knit.
Row 3: K2tog, knit to last stitch, p1. (25 stitches)
Row 4: Knit.
Row 5-10: Repeat rows 3-4 three times. (22 stitches)
Row 11: Knit to last stitch, p1.
BO remaining 22 stitches.

*Sleeves (make 2)*

*For Flower Petal hem, with CC, CO 3 stitches.
Row 1 (RS): Knit.
Row 2 (WS): K1, yo, k1, yo, k1. (5 stitches)
Row 3 and all RS rows: Knit.
Row 4: K1, yo, k3, yo, k1. (7 stitches)
Row 6: K1, yo, k2tog, k1, ssk, yo, k1. (7 stitches)
Row 7: Knit.
Row 8: Knit.
Break yarn. Leave on RH needle.
Repeat from * for 7 more petals. Do not break yarn after last petal.
Row 9: Knit across all petals to join. (56 stitches)
Row 10: CO 1 stitch, knit to end. (57 stitches)
Row 11: CO 1 stitch, knit to end. (58 stitches)
Row 12: P1, knit to last stitch, p1.
Row 13: Knit.
Repeat rows 12-13 until piece measures 6¾" (17cm) from joining row at top of petals. BO all stitches.

*Drawstring*

With CC and double pointed needles, CO 6 stitches. Work 60" (152cm) of I-cord. BO.

## Bonnet

With MC, CO 56 stitches. Work in garter stitch for 40 rows (20 ridges).

*Back flap*

Row 1: BO 18, k1, k2tog, k14, k2tog, k19. (36 stitches)

Row 2: BO 18, knit to end. (18 stitches)
Row 3: K1, k2tog, knit to last 3 stitches, k2tog, k1. (16 stitches)
Row 4: Knit.
Row 5: Same as row 3. (14 stitches)
Row 6-30: Knit.
Row 31: K1, k2tog, knit to last 3 stitches, k2tog, k1. (12 stitches)
Row 32: Knit.
Row 33-36: Repeat row 31-32 twice. (8 stitches)
Row 37-40: Knit.
BO all stitches.

*Bonnet petal trim*
*With CC, CO 3 stitches.
Row 1 (RS): Knit.
Row 2 (WS): K1, yo, k1, yo, k1. (5 stitches)
Row 3 and all RS rows: Knit.
Row 4: K1, yo, k3, yo, k1. (7 stitches)
Row 6 & 8: K1, yo, k2tog, k1, ssk, yo, k1. (7 stitches)
Row 9-10: Knit.
Break yarn. Leave on RH needle.
Repeat from * for 5 more petals. Do not break yarn after last petal.
Row 11: Knit across all petals to join. (42 stitches)
Row 12: Knit. Break yarn. Leave on needle.

*Face edge*
Row 1 (RS): With right side facing and MC, pick up and knit 56 stitches along face edge.
Row 2 (WS): Knit.
Row 3: K7 stitches from bonnet needle. Holding the petal trim in front of the bonnet edge, and continuing with MC, knit one stitch of the petal trim from the front needle together with one stitch of the bonnet. Join all bonnet petal trim stitches. Knit remaining 7 stitches from bonnet needle. (56 stitches)
Row 4: Knit.
Row 5: K1f&b, work in 1x1 rib to last stitch, k1f&b. (58 stitches)
Row 6: Keeping in pattern, work 1x1 rib.
Row 7: K1f&b, keeping in pattern work 1x1 rib until the last stitch, k1f&b. (60 stitches)
BO in rib.

*Neck edge*
Stitch back seams of bonnet.
Row 1 (RS): With right side facing and MC, pick up and knit 48 stitches along neck edge, not picking up any stitches from the ribbing at the face edge.

Row 2: K1f&b, work in 1x1 rib to last stitch, k1f&b. (50 stitches)
Row 3: Keeping in pattern, work 1x1 rib.
Row 4: K1f&b, keeping in pattern work 1x1 rib until the last stitch, k1f&b. (52 stitches)
BO in rib.

*Ties (make 2)*
With MC and double pointed needles, CO 4 stitches. Work I-cord for 7" (18cm). BO.

## Finishing

*Bunting*
Weave in ends. Block pieces to dimension in blocking chart on page 149. Stitch shoulder seams. With outside facing and CC, pick up and knit 51 stitches along neck. Work 3 rows of 1x1 rib. BO in rib. Mark center of sleeve bind off edge. Matching center of sleeve to shoulder seam, stitch sleeve to body. Repeat for second sleeve. Sew side seam from hem to sleeve opening on each side. Whipstitch both edges of both sides of snap tape to flanges of front, from neck ribbing to bottom of flange, taking care to line up snaps. Weave the drawstring through the eyelets below flanges. Knot each end of the drawstring.

*Bonnet*
Whipstitch the face edge ribbing to neck edge ribbing. Stitch the ties to front corners.
*Optional:* Cut 6 strands of MC 6" (15cm) long. Hold 3 strands together and fold in half. Using crochet hook, apply as fringe to the bottom end of each tie. Trim the ends even. Tie a half hitch knot at the bottom of the tie just above the fringe.

## Tips

- You may find it easier to weave in the ends on the petals after knitting the two joining rows and before the trim is knit to the body of the bonnet or bunting.
- If you prefer, you can eliminate the eyelet row and drawstring on the bunting and stitch snaps individually or with snap tape above the hem petals as a closure, or leave the bottom completely open.
- Knit the entire piece in white for a snowy christening gown covering.

## Alabama and the Camellia

The camellia may not have been Alabama's first state flower, but it has certainly been their favorite. Alabamans have celebrated their love affair with camellias by putting its name on everything from restaurants to beauty pageants to their government's online help system. The state has many beautiful public gardens where you can experience this elegant flower for yourself:

*Bellingrath Gardens and Home*, Theodore, Mobile County - This 10,500 square foot home and its 65 acre garden are open year round. The home, built in 1935, is filled with the original furnishings. Directions and hours can be found online at Bellingrath.org.

*Dothan Area Botanical Gardens*, Dothan - This municipal garden boasts 15 specialty areas, including one dedicated to camellias. The Southern Heirloom Garden features varieties of plants collected from historic home sites. The gardens are online at ExploreSouthernHistory.com.

*Arlington Antebellum Home and Gardens*, Birmingham - Built in 1845, the plantation home is surrounded by 6 acres of beautiful Southern gardens. The Gothic Revival mansion is home to a lovely collection of 19th-century furniture and decorative arts.

*Aldridge Gardens*, Hoover - Formerly the estate of horticulturist Eddie Aldridge and his wife, the house and 30 acres of woodland gardens now belong to the city of Hoover and are open to the public. On display in the gardens are over 40 varieties of camellias. You can find more information at AldridgeGardens.com.

# Mardi Gras Party Bangles

Mobile, Alabama

*Mention "Mardi Gras" and New Orleans immediately springs to mind. But America's oldest celebration is in the city of Mobile. More family-friendly than debauched drinking spree, it's a great chance to party with or without your kids, since unlike its Creole cousin, at Mobile's Mardi Gras everyone stays clothed!*

*Mardi Gras beads, best worn in large numbers, are the inspiration for these fun felted bangles. A great stash-busting project, each bracelet uses about 25 yards of sport weight wool and however many size 6/0 glass beads you want. Inexpensive hard plastic bangles are used as a "resist" sewn into the simple, flat-knit piece. Then the whole thing is tossed into the washing machine and voilà— it's Mardi Gras Madness for your wrists. They're fast and fabulous for gift knitting as well.*

## About this Project

**Skill Level:** Easy

**Finished Size:** Will fit most wrists; after felting, bracelet inside circumference is about 8" (20cm) and width is approximately 3/4" (1.75cm)

**Project Gauge:** 28 stitches and 40 rows = approximately 4" (10cm) before felting

## Stitch Guide

*Pb (place bead)*
Knit to stitch to be beaded. Bring yarn to front. Push bead up to right hand needle. Slip the stitch to be beaded purlwise with yarn in front. Bring yarn to back and knit the next stitch, pulling the beaded "collar" around the slipped stitch, making sure to keep bead to the front of the work, and snug it to the stitch.

## Instructions

Thread desired number of beads onto yarn. CO 12 stitches (see *Tips* for instructions for other sizes of plastic bangles). Work in stockinette stitch (knit on RS, purl on WS) until piece measures 12" (30cm). Use the "pb" technique above to place beads as desired. When changing colors, either carry the unused color up the side or cut the yarn and tie the next color to the old color with a knot. Repeat for each bracelet. BO, leaving a 24" (60cm) tail.

## Finishing

Do not weave in ends. If you have loose ends that were not previously tied, do that now. Trim ends to 1" (1.25cm) other than BO tail. Thread BO tail through tapestry needle. Using mattress stitch, stitch side edges of the knitting together, enclosing the plastic bangle as you go. The knitting will be longer than the bracelet, so just push the finished part together slightly to keep it out of your way as you work. Then mattress stitch the open ends of the tube together, making sure the side seam is lined up. Knot last stitch and run end up through inside of bracelet. Trim end. Move the seam to the inside edge of the bracelet. Set washing machine on hottest temperature. Add a small amount of laundry soap. If your washer allows, turn off the spin cycle. Put the bracelets in the washer with a few light-colored towels for friction. Put through a short cycle and check felting. Repeat cycle until fully felted and knitting is tight to the plastic bracelet. Remove from washer and place on paper towels and allow to dry completely.

## Shopping List

Cascade Yarns *220 Wool Sport* (100% wool, 163 yards/150m); approximately 25 yards (22.5m) for each bracelet; shown in Cerise #7802, Purple Hyacinth #7808, Orange Sherbet #7825, Goldenrod #7827, Cyan Blue #8891, and Primavera #8903

Size US 6 (4mm) needles

Glass 6/0 beads

Beading needle

Tapestry needle

Hard plastic bracelet in size and width desired (bracelet shown is 11" (28cm) outer circumference and approximately 1/2" (1.25cm) wide (see *Tips* for adapting this pattern to other bracelet sizes)

## Tips

- You may be tempted to put all the beads on the yarn at once, but restrain yourself. The yarn is slightly damaged by pushing the beads along and if you put too many beads on, it may break the yarn. If you need more, just break the yarn at the end of a row, string on more and tie the yarn back together.
- When deciding where to place beads, it helps keep the felted fabric firm if you don't put them directly above each other on two consecutive right side rows. Instead, either work a couple of rows of stockinette between, or offset them by moving the next RS row beading over a stitch or two.
- Before felting the bracelet, check to make sure all beads are sitting on the outside. If any have wiggled to the inside, push them back through the knitting and center them on their little collars.
- If you want to cover a different size bracelet, here's the proportion: for the circumference, measure the outside edge of the bracelet and add 10% to get the total length of the knitting. For width, measure the circumference of bracelet plastic by wrapping a tape measure from inside to outside and back to inside to measure how much width the knitting needs to cover when it's stitched into a tube; multiply by 1.75 to get the width in inches of the required knitting.

Mardi Gras is one of my favorite celebrations. We host a huge party in our home every year with live music and beads by the bucketful. Our guests pile on the beads and I'm always amazed by how some of them can stand upright under the weight!

# Sweet Tea

*Here in the South, we take our tea seriously. It's the only place where you order iced tea, and they always have to ask, "Is that sweet or unsweet?" Of course the perfect iced tea is smooth, full-bodied, and above all else— sweet. If you're serving afternoon drinks in the summer, don't dare consider using an artificial sweetener. Just a tall glass of tradition, please!*

## Directions

Add desired amount of sugar to 3-4 cups of water and bring just to a boil. Stir to make sure sugar is completely dissolved. Add a pinch of baking soda to the water (removes bitterness) and add 3 large, family-sized tea bags or 8-10 regular sized. Most sweet tea connoisseurs swear by Luzianne©, but Lipton© Iced Tea Brew will do. Remove from heat and cover. Do not continue to boil after the tea bags are added.

Steep for least 15 minutes and up to an hour. Remove tea bags. Pour into a 1 gallon pitcher and add cold water to desired strength and refrigerate. If tea is still warm and to be served immediately, instead of water, fill rest of the pitcher with ice.

Keeps in refrigerator for a week, but really best if consumed in a couple of days.

## Shopping List

1 to 1½ cups granulated sugar

3 to 4 cups of water

3 large, family-sized tea bags (or 8-10 regular sized)

If you can't decide between a trip to majestic mountains or the peaceful seashore, North Carolina should be your destination of choice. With hiking, skiing, sunbathing and over 300 miles of coastline all wrapped up in one place, you never have to choose.

Western North Carolina is all about mountains, with the Smoky and Blue Ridge ranges providing stunning scenery year round. During the summer, cool mountain air lures refugees from the Southern heat, and lush snowfalls make for top-notch skiing in the winter months. George Washington Vanderbilt II was so taken with North Carolina's natural beauty, he built the world's largest private home, Biltmore, in Asheville. The mansion stands watch over a spectacular array of woods, hills and lakes. The Blue Ridge Parkway winds through these mountains, one of the most scenic drives in the U.S. It's one of my favorite places in the world.

From Wilmington up to the Outer Banks, the Carolina coast is a great place to enjoy the "4 S's" of a perfect beach vacation— sun, sand, surf and seafood. The Eastern Seaboard's highest sand dunes, warm waters and wind-swept barrier islands are just a few of the state's unforgettable features.

History buffs will find much to discover in North Carolina. The Museum of the Cherokee Indian, in the city of Cherokee, tells the tale of that tribe's 10,000 year history. You can also visit Roanoke Island, site of the first English settlement in the New World. The Fort Raleigh National Historic Site tells the island's story, including the mysterious disappearance of those early English settlers. The aviation age was born in North Carolina when the Wright Brothers launched Flyer I from Kill Devil Hills. A museum and reconstructed hangar celebrate their achievement. For more recent history, the Topsail Island Museum documents a secret government missile program on the quiet island in the 1940s.

Whether you visit for the mountains, the beaches, or the museums, you'll be sure to take a bit of North Carolina home in your heart.

# North Carolina

# Gilded Age Placemats

Asheville, North Carolina

*Biltmore, perched in the Smoky Mountains at Asheville, North Carolina, is the country's largest private home and a stunning remnant of the Gilded Age of steel tycoons and robber barons. These placemats are a nod to the glittering table settings of that time, but with a modern twist—surreal flatware designs and metallic yarns. So set your table and get a little glam for yourself, even if dinner comes straight from the microwave rather than from silver salvers.*

*This project is worked in "stranded intarsia"— stranding the background color behind the contrast color only. The result is a double layer of yarn in the flatware design elements, but a single layer for the background, giving a slightly raised appearance that helps set them apart from the background.*

## About this Project

**Skill Level:** Intermediate

**Finished Size:** Approximately 20" (50cm) wide by 13" (33cm) high

**Project Gauge:** 24 stitches and 32 rows = 4" (10cm) in stockinette stitch

*Note:* Gauge is not critical but will impact the finished size and the amount of yarn used.

## Shopping List

Berroco *Metallic FX* (85% rayon, 15% metallic, 85 yards/78m); 2 skeins each Gold #1001 (MC) and Silver #1002 (CC) for each placemat

Size US 8 (5mm) needles

Tapestry needle

Fray stopping liquid

1/2 yard (.5m) white commercial felt fabric (will line 3 placemats)

White sewing thread and sewing needle

## Stitch Guide

*Stranded intarsia*
Use butterflies of yarn for contrast color (CC) flatware elements. Carry background yarn (MC) loosely behind, catching floats every 3-4 stitches. Do not strand the CC behind the background of the placemat.

## Instructions

With CC, loosely and evenly CO 110 stitches. Work eleven rows of garter stitch (knitting every row). Knit next row, placing marker after 8 stitches and then 8 stitches before end. Bottom border completed.

*Begin charted design*
With CC, knit 8 stitches. Drop CC, but do not cut. Join MC, and continue with chart row 1 to last 8 stitches. Join a second ball of CC and with CC only, work remaining 8 stitches in garter stitch. The first and last 8 stitches of every row are worked in garter stitch with CC. The stitches between markers are worked in stockinette stitch (knit on the RS, purl on the WS) according to chart. Continue working chart, joining butterflies of CC for the designs as needed, keeping 8 stitches on both ends in garter stitch with CC, and working flatware designs in "*stranded intarsia*" technique in CC until charted rows are complete. Drop MC and with CC only, work 12 rows of garter stitch. BO very loosely and evenly.

## Finishing

Weave in ends. After cutting excess tail, place a drop of fray stopping liquid at the end and allow to dry completely. Block placemat to finished size. When placemat is dry, it will be slightly off square. Cut felt 1/2" (1.25cm) shorter and narrower than the widest measurements of the dry placemat. Center felt on back of placemat. Pin each corner, one stitch in from knitted edges. Then pin along all edges, bringing knitted edge up so lining is one stitch in from edge all the way around. Using blanket stitch or whipstitch and doubled white sewing thread, stitch lining to back of placemat, being careful not to sew through the knitted stitches on the front of the placemat.

The epitome of Gilded Age opulence, Biltmore's home and gardens provide those of us who don't own railroads or steel mills a glimpse of an extraordinary life and time.

## Tips

- A tight cast on or bind off will ruin this project. If you work too tightly, go up one or two needle sizes.
- For a more interesting tabletop, make half the placemats as shown and half in reverse color.
- This yarn is pretty slippery after winding. Drop the ball of the background color in a highball or juice glass to keep it from unraveling. Grab a second glass while you're at it and fill it with something yummy over ice....

"Stranded intarsia" creates dimension in the design elements by carrying the background yarn behind the contrast color used for the flatware pattern, as shown in this photo.

*Placemat Chart*

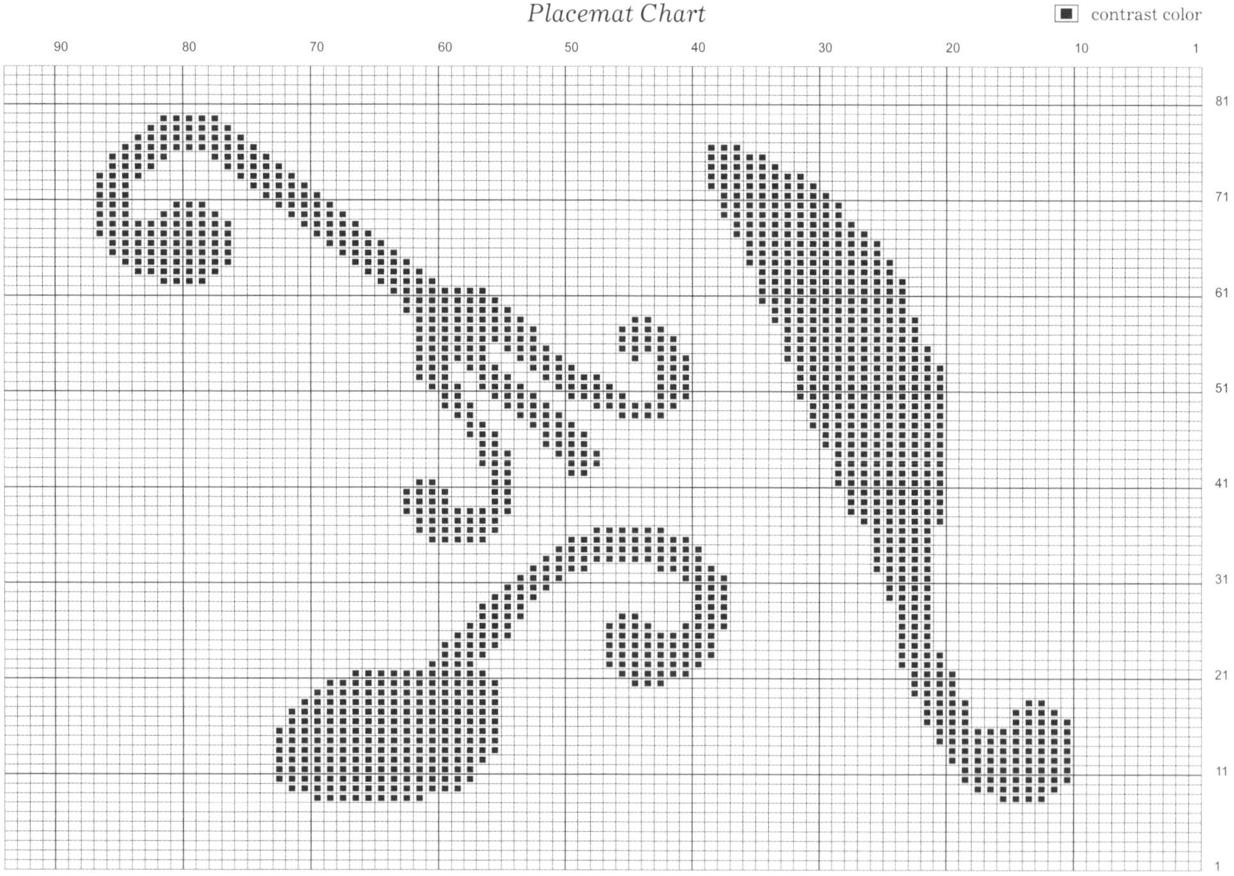

■ contrast color

## How to Live Like a Robber Baron

Biltmore may be the largest Gilded Age home in the South, but it's by no means the only one. The advent of train travel in the late 19th century made it possible for Northern industrialists to create their own odes to excess all over the warmer Southern states. Plus, the South had its own native "robber barons," who built personal palaces to rival their part-time neighbors from the North. Many of these homes are open to the public and all provide a jaw-dropping reminder of a time and lifestyle long since gone.

*Reynolda House Museum of American Art*, Winston-Salem - Built in 1917 as a vacation home for R.J. Reynolds, founder of the tobacco company that still bears his name, this house was the centerpiece of an estate spanning more than 1,000 acres. It opened as a museum in 1967 and features several rooms restored to reflect the era when the Reynolds family occupied the home. The grounds include twenty-eight of the original thirty buildings, now housing shops and restaurants, as well as restored formal gardens. More information is available at ReynoldaHouse.org.

*Whitehall*, Palm Beach - Oil, real estate, and railroad magnate Henry Flagler built a railroad all the way to Miami just to make his winter getaways a little more convenient. Flagler is responsible for several stunningly opulent hotels along Florida's coast, including the landmark Breakers in Palm Beach. In 1902 he built his personal residence, Whitehall, instantly transforming Palm Beach into the official winter playground for the super-rich. At 60,000 square feet, the Whitehall mansion is larger than the White House! Now housing the Flagler Museum, all 55 rooms of this Beaux Arts gem are fully decorated with period furnishings. The private rail car he and his wife used for their annual trip south is also on display in an annex. Now completely restored with the original marble floors and walls, ceiling murals, and heavy gilding, the home is listed as a National Historic Landmark. You can find more information at FlaglerMuseum.us.

*Vizcaya*, Miami - Traveling further south along the route first opened by Flagler's Florida East Coast Railway, Miami and its 1916 robber baron showcase Vizcaya await. At the time it was built, 10% of Miami's population was employed in its construction. Commissioned as a winter residence by industrialist James Deering, the mansion was designed to appear as if it had been standing for 400 years, with each passing (imagined) generation renovating the home. Instant history, anyone? Damaged and repaired after numerous hurricanes, Deering's heirs eventually sold the house, extensive gardens, and most of the land to Dade County. The furnishings were donated for as long as the grounds remain a museum. You can find Vizcaya online at VizcayaMuseum.org.

# Cherokee Vest

Franklin, North Carolina

*Long before European settlers arrived in the mountains around Franklin, North Carolina, the foothills were home to the Cherokee Nation, who called the area "Nikwasi," the Cherokee word for "star." You'll be a "Nikwasi" yourself in this lovely vest from* ***Kristin Murphy*** *of* ***Silver Threads & Golden Needles****. The design is inspired by traditional Native American patterns, but knit in a modern natural color palette. Intended to be worn as shown, you can choose to knit a larger size for a less open look. It complements a wide range of body shapes and its long, lean lines will make you look taller and slimmer. It's mountain magic.*

## About this Project

**Skill Level:** Easy-mediate

**Fit Tip:** This vest is designed to be worn open. Choose your size depending on your preference for styling. Patricia is wearing a Medium.

**Finished Sizes:** S (M, L) with finished bust measurements of 34 (38, 42)" [86 (97, 107)cm] with vest open

**Project Gauge:** 16 stitches and 24 rows = 4" (10cm) in stockinette stitch

## Shopping List

Blue Sky Alpacas *Worsted Cotton* (100% organic cotton, 150yds/137m); 3 (4, 5) skeins Stone #626, 2 skeins Toffee #623, 1 skein Fern #620

Size US 8 (5mm) 32" (81cm) or longer circular needle

Size US 8 (5mm) 16" (40cm) circular needle for armhole trim

Stitch markers

Stitch holders

Tapestry needle

## Instructions

*Body*
With Toffee and longer needle, CO 144 (160, 176) stitches.
Row 1-10: Knit. Change to Stone.
Row 11 (RS): Knit.
Row 12 (WS): Purl.
Repeat row 11-12 until piece measures 10 (10½, 11)" [25 (27, 28)cm] from cast on edge, ending with a WS row.
Next row (RS): K36 (40, 44), pm, k72 (80, 88), pm, knit to end.
Next row (WS): Purl.
Next (decrease) row: Knit to marker, slip marker, ssk, knit to 2 stitches before next marker, k2tog, slip marker, knit to end.
Next row: Purl.
Repeat last 2 rows 7 times. 128 (144, 160) stitches.
*Armhole shaping*
K20 (22, 24), BO 20 stitches for underarm, k47 (59, 71) [48 (60, 72) back stitches including last stitch of bind off], BO 20 stitches for underarm, knit to end.

*Left front*
Next row (WS): P20 (22, 24), place remaining stitches on a holder. Working these 20 (22, 24) stitches only, knit 1 row, purl 1 row. Join Toffee and work 4 rows in stockinette stitch.
*Begin charted design*
Row 1 (RS): K0 (1, 2), work row 1 of chart, k0 (1, 2).
Row 2 (WS): P0 (1, 2), work row 2 of chart, p0 (1, 2).
Continuing as established, work all rows of chart twice. Place stitches on holder.

*Right front*
With WS facing, join Stone and work as for left front.

*Back*
With WS facing, join Stone and work 3 rows in stockinette stitch, ending with a WS row. Join Toffee and work 4 rows in stockinette stitch.

*Begin charted design*
Row 1 (RS): K0 (1, 2), work row 1 of chart, k0 (1, 2); with Toffee, knit to last 20 (22, 24) stitches; k0 (1, 2), work row 1 of chart, k0 (1, 2).
Row 2 (WS): P0 (1, 2), work row 2 of chart, p0 (1, 2); with Toffee, purl to last 20 (22, 24) stitches; p0 (1, 2), work row 2 of chart, p0 (1, 2). Continuing as established, work all rows of chart once. On last row, BO center 8 (16, 24) stitches for back neck. Working each side separately, repeat chart pattern on first and last 20 (22, 24) stitches once more. Cut yarn, leaving a long tail for 3-needle bind off.

*Cherokee Vest Chart*

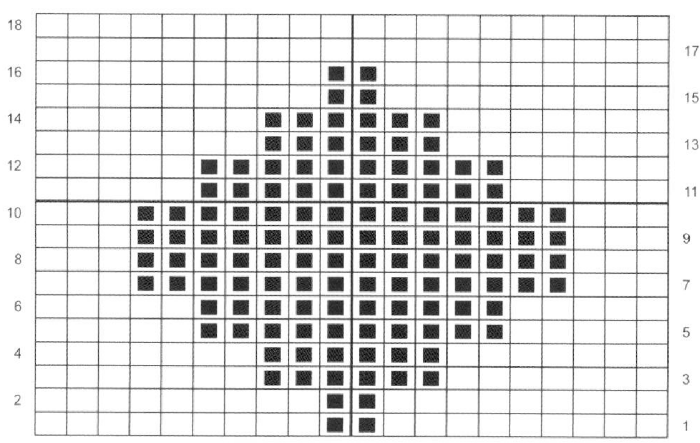

## Finishing

Join shoulders using 3-needle bind off.

*Front trim*
With RS facing, longer needle and Toffee, starting at bottom left front edge, pick up and knit three out of every four stitches around left front, neck and right front of vest. Knit seven rows. BO all stitches.

*Armhole trim*
With RS facing, shorter needle and Toffee, pick up and knit three out of every four stitches around armhole. Place marker and join.
Round 1: Purl.
Round 2: Knit.
Round 3-4: Repeat rounds 1-2.
BO pwise.

Weave in ends. Block according to chart on page 150.

*Silver Threads & Golden Needles* is owned by mother and daughter duo *Virginia Murphy and Kristin McDougall,* and their best friend *Amy Murphy.* You can find them in Franklin's historic downtown and at SilverThreadsYarn.com.

# Creamy Sweet Potato Pie

*The Southern cousin to pumpkin pie, sweet potatoes make for a dense, rich filling. This version lightens the texture to create a divinely smooth, almost delicate dessert. Perfect on its own or with a dollop of sweetened whipped cream, you can still count it as a serving of veggies!*

## Directions

*Sweet Pie Crust*
Makes a single crust for a 9" pie pan.

Mix the dry ingredients in a large mixing bowl. Using your fingers, mix the cold butter and vegetable shortening into the flour mixture, rubbing it between your fingers to crumble the shortening into coarse crumbs. Add just enough ice water to form a dough. Work the dough as little as possible. Overworking the dough will result in a tough, heavy crust. Turn the dough out of the bowl, shape into a thick, flat disk, wrap tightly in plastic wrap, and refrigerate for at least 30 minutes. On a lightly floured surface and using a floured rolling pin, roll from the center out to fit a 9" pie pan. Transfer to the ungreased pie pan, cover with plastic wrap and chill until ready to fill.

*Sweet Potato Filling*
Bake or microwave sweet potatoes until soft, then peel and mash. Let cool completely. In a separate bowl, whip egg whites until soft peaks form. In a separate bowl, lightly beat the egg yolks. Add milk to egg yolks and beat, then add melted butter. Add egg yolk mixture to the cooled mashed potatoes and mix well. Add remaining ingredients, except for the egg whites. Beat until almost smooth, leaving some very small chunks of sweet potato in the filling. Gently fold in the whipped egg whites.

*Baking Instructions*
Preheat oven to 350 degrees. Spoon the sweet potato mixture into the 9" unbaked pie crust. Smooth to make an even layer. Place pie pan on a cookie sheet. Bake for 50-60 minutes, or until the center is set. Cool.

Serve with a dollop of sweetened whipped cream on top. For a classic holiday treat, top with marshmallows and broil until melted and lightly browned.

## Shopping List

*Sweet Pie Crust*

- 6 Tbl very cold unsalted butter, cut into small pieces
- 2 Tbl very cold vegetable shortening
- 1 1/4 cups all purpose flour
- 1 Tbl sugar
- 1/4 tsp salt
- 3 to 4 Tbls cold water

*Sweet Potato Filling*

- 1 pound sweet potatoes, baked or microwaved
- 1/2 cup butter, melted
- 1/2 cup granulated sugar
- 1/2 cup brown sugar
- 3/4 cup milk
- 2 eggs, separated
- 2 1/2 tsp pumpkin pie spice
- 1 tsp pure vanilla extract

You see a picture of gorgeously detailed wrought iron gates. Quick, what's the first place you think of? I'm betting it's Charleston. No images are more iconic of the old South than the cobblestone streets, flickering gas lamps, ornate wrought iron gates and delicate fences and window boxes of Charleston's Old City.

Almost 350 years old, Charleston has survived fires, hurricanes, earthquakes, pirates, two wars, and worse— millions of tourists in plaid shorts and striped shirts. The city was established by English settlers in 1670 and 73 pre-Revolutionary War buildings stand to this day, along with another 750 dating from before the Civil War. You can experience centuries of American history up close, since many of these buildings are open for tours. Of special note is Middleton Place, a nearly 300 year old plantation, where you can tour the oldest landscaped gardens in America.

Ready for a little shopping? Charleston's historic City Market has four blocks of open air stalls, modeled after The Temple of the Wingless Victory, in Athens (Greece, not Georgia). It was built in 1841 and the market, shopping, restaurants and gullah women— singing and weaving Charleston's famous sweetgrass baskets— are not to be missed. The market is one of the oldest in the country.

Charleston's Old Slave Mart Museum documents a very different kind of historical market. The last slave market building standing in South Carolina, the museum displays African American history and art, while recounting the state's role as a center for domestic slave trading.

For more history, take a ferry to Sullivan's Island in Charleston harbor to visit the sites of two major American conflicts. The Civil War's first full-scale battle took place at Fort Sumter on April 12, 1861, when Confederate artillery opened fire on the fort. Nearby, Fort Moultrie was the location of the first American victory over the British Navy, in 1776. Both forts have museums and education centers.

Whether it's history, architecture or the romance of gas lamps and cobblestones you're after, come to Charleston. I'll see you there!

# Gracious Lace Tea Towel

Aiken, South Carolina

*The custom of afternoon tea is part of the graciousness of the Deep South, whether the tea is served from Great-Grandma's wedding silver or in a tall glass of ice, garnished with fresh mint. No lady worth her white gloves and low-heeled pumps would be caught dead serving instant tea (perish the thought!) or serving her afternoon callers tea without a lovely lace-trimmed tea towel.*

*This knitted confection from* **Barbara Sue Brodie Needleworks** *in Aiken, South Carolina is embroidered in duplicate stitch with your family initial. It adds a bit of true Southern charm, even if the tea you're serving is in South Dakota rather than South Carolina.*

## About this Project

**Skill Level:** Easy-mediate

**Finished Size:** Approximately 9.5" wide by 30" long (24cm x 75cm)

**Project Gauge:** 26 stitches and 30 rows = 4" (10cm) in stockinette stitch

## Stitch Guide

*Seeded Background Stitch*
Row 1 (RS): P1, *k3, p1; repeat from * to end.
Row 2 (WS): Purl.
Row 3: Knit.
Row 4: Purl.
Row 5: K2, *p1, k3; repeat from * to last 3 stitches, p1, k2.
Row 6: Purl.
Row 7: Knit.
Row 8: Purl.

*Lace Stitch*
Row 1: K2, (k1, p1, k1) in the same stitch, yo, p4tog, k1, (yo) twice, k2tog, (yo) twice, k2. (15 stitches)
Row 2: Sl1 wyif, (k2, p1) twice, k2, (k1, p1, k1) in the same stitch, yo, p4tog, k1. (15 stitches)
Row 3: K2, (k1, p1, k1) in the same stitch, yo, p4tog, k8. (15 stitches)
Row 4: BO 3, k5 (6 stitches on needle including stitch left after BO), (k1, p1, k1) in the same stitch, yo, p4tog, k1. (12 stitches)
Repeat rows 1-4 until desired length.

## Instructions

CO 61 stitches.
Row 1-8: Work 8 rows of *Seeded Background Stitch.*
Row 9-15: Repeat rows 1-7.
Row 16: Knit.
Row 17: Place removable marker in first stitch to mark beginning of monogram band section. Knit.
Row 18: Purl.
Row 19-36: Repeat rows 17-18 nine times (do not continue to add additional stitch markers).
Row 37: Knit. Place removable marker in last stitch to mark end of monogram band section.
Row 38: Knit.
Row 39-44: Work rows 3-8 of *Seeded Background Stitch.*

### Shopping List

Louet *Euroflax Sport* (100% wet spun linen, 270 yards/245m); 2 skeins Cream #30

Approximately 3 yards (2.75m) contrasting sportweight yarn for monogram

Size US 3 (3.25mm) needles

Removable stitch markers

Tapestry needle

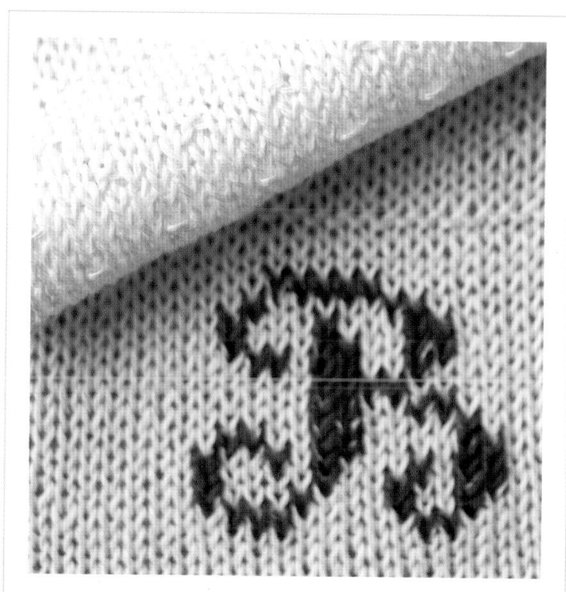

Row 45-172: Repeat rows 1-8 of *Seeded Background Stitch* sixteen times. Piece should measure approximately 22-23" (56-58cm) from CO edge.
BO all stitches.

*Lace trim*
CO 11 stitches.
Setup row: K9, yo, k2. (12 stitches)
Work four rows of *Lace Stitch*. Repeat rows 1-4 of *Lace Stitch* until piece measures length of short edge of towel. BO all stitches. Repeat for second short edge of towel.

*Lace Stitch Chart*

| Row | | | | | | | | | | | | | | Row |
|---|---|---|---|---|---|---|---|---|---|---|---|---|---|---|
| 4 | ■ | ∩ | ∩ | ∩ | ● | ● | ● | ● | ● | V̇ | O | Λ4 | ● | |
| | | | | | | | | | Λ4 | O | V̇ | | | 3 |
| 2 | V | ● | ● | | ● | ● | | ● | ● | V̇ | O | Λ4 | ● | |
| | | | O | O | / | O | O | | Λ4 | O | V̇ | | | 1 |

- □ RS: knit; WS: purl
- V̇ RS and WS: (k1, p1, k1) in same stitch
- O RS and WS: yarnover
- Λ4 RS: p4tog
- / RS: k2tog
- ● RS: purl; WS: knit
- Λ4 WS: p4tog
- V WS: Sl1 pwise wyif
- ∩ WS: bind off
- ■ placeholder - no stitch

## Finishing

Weave in ends. Block towel. Block lace to match width of the towel, pinning out points. Allow to dry completely. With right sides together, whipstitch lace to towel ends.

*Duplicate stitch monogram*
Center the monogram vertically and horizontally on the monogram band. Duplicate stitch monogram using contrasting yarn.

## Tips

- The chart for the lace looks like there are only 13 rather than 15 stitches on the needle at the end of rows 1-3. However, remember that lace charts show *actions*, rather than actual *stitches*. Because of the increases and decreases, the chart is correct.
- On the lace trim, the (k1, p1, k1) in the same stitch will always be worked in the yarnover of the row below.
- When making the yarnover in between a knit and purl stitch, make sure you're creating a full yarnover loop and not just pulling the yarn between the needles. Check out our Planet Purl video for yarnovers and double yarnovers to learn how to do a yarnover between knit and purl stitches.
- If you like a little sparkle, use a metallic yarn for the monogram. You can also add beads to the trim by stringing beads onto a length of the linen yarn and placing the beads along the edge of the trim using slip stitch crochet and a small crochet hook. Or go for the glam and do both!

*Barbara Sue Brodie's* shop is located in historic Aiken, South Carolina, where you can tour historic mansions that were built during Aiken's days as a Winter Colony for wealthy Northerners. You can find the shop online at BarbaraSueBrodie.com.

## Monogram Chart

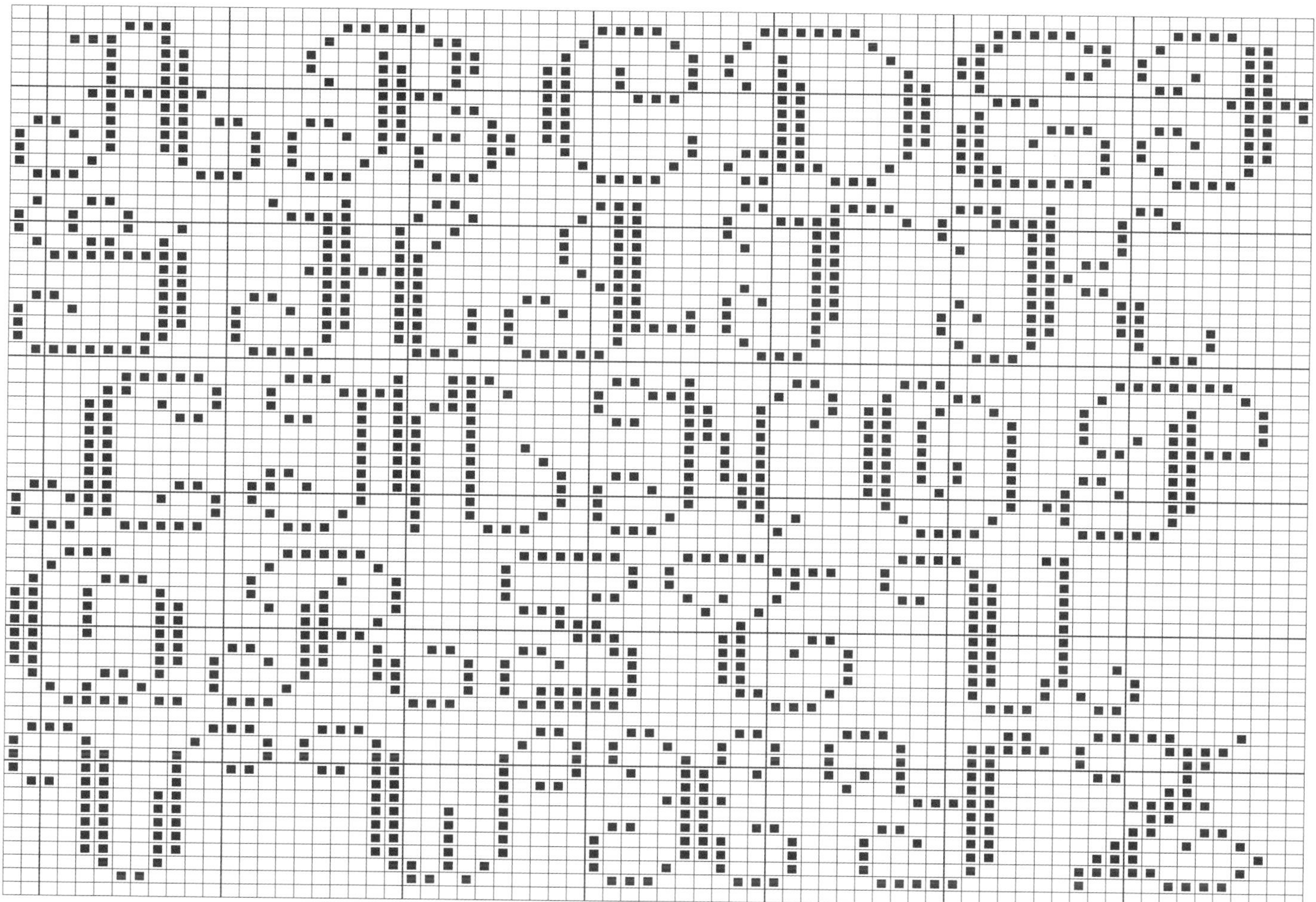

■ contrast color

# Wrought Iron Gate Pillows

## Charleston, South Carolina

Charleston has a singular and sophisticated culture that has survived from its founding in 1670 through the American Revolution, Civil War and into the present.

While the city has long been safe from rampaging Redcoats, many of the old buildings' magnificent wrought iron gates still stand, now protecting South Carolina's oldest city and its inhabitants from door-to-door salesmen (if nothing else). Those gates inspired this elegant set of throw pillows, featuring the designs of a scroll, a lyre and perhaps the city's most famous wrought iron masterpiece, the Swordgate.

These knitted gates may not keep out unwanted suitors, or guests who overstay their welcome, but they will definitely gussy up your favorite chaise, divan or fainting couch.

## About this Project

**Skill Level:** Intermediate

**Finished Sizes (without trim):** Beige - 12" (30cm) high by 16"(40cm) wide; Blue - 18" (45cm) high by 14" (35cm) wide; Rose - 16" (40cm) square

**Project Gauge:** 20 stitches and 28 rows = 4" (10cm) in stockinette stitch on Size US 7 (4.5mm) needles after blocking

*Note:* The stranded pattern on the front will knit at a slightly tighter gauge. The back of the pillow has been adjusted to accommodate the tighter gauge of the stranded front.

## Stitch Guide

*Wrought Iron Lace*
Begin with 5 stitches CO.
Row 1: K3, yo twice, k2. (7 stitches)
Row 2: K3, p1, k2, p1. (7 stitches)
Row 3: Knit. (7 stitches)
Row 4: BO 2 stitches, k3, p1. (5 stitches)
Repeat rows 1-4 until desired length.

*Ribbed Edge Stitch*
Row 1: P1, *k2, p2; repeat from * to last stitch, p1.
Row 2: K1, *p2, k2; repeat from * to last stitch, k1.
Repeat rows 1-2.

## Instructions

*Note:* Instructions are given for Beige (Blue, Rose) pillow

*Pillow front*
With MC, CO 85 (65, 75) stitches. Knit one row, placing marker after stitch 12 (5, 8) and stitch 73 (60, 67). Work an additional 5 (6, 9) rows in stockinette stitch in MC, knitting all stitches on the RS and purling all stitches on the WS for a total of 6 (7, 10 rows).
*Charted section*
The 61 (55, 59) stitches between the markers are worked according to the chart, with the stitches outside the markers worked in the MC only. Work all rows of the chart in stockinette stitch, using stranded technique, knitting odd numbered rows working right to left and purling even numbered rows, working left to right. When all charted rows are complete, discontinue CC and work additional 6 (7, 10) rows of stockinette stitch in MC only. Total 65 (95, 93) rows. BO all stitches.

*Pillow back (make 2 for each pillow)*
With MC, CO 78 (58, 70) stitches. Work 54 (90, 70) rows of stockinette stitch, ending with a wrong side row. Work 6 rows of *Ribbed Edge Stitch.* BO in ribbing.

## Shopping List

*Beige pillow*

Cascade Yarns *220 Wool* (100% wool, 220 yards/200m); 2 skeins Beige #8021 (MC), half skein Black #8555 (CC)

Small amount of worsted weight bright yellow yarn

12" (30cm) x 16" (40cm) pillow form

*Blue pillow*

Cascade Yarns *220 Wool* (100% wool, 220 yards/200m); 2 skeins Anis #8908 (MC), half skein Black #8555 (CC)

14" (45cm) x 18" (35cm) pillow form

Size US 7 (4.5mm) double pointed needles

*Rose pillow*

Cascade Yarns *220 Wool* (100% wool, 220 yards/200m); 2 skeins Medium Rose #8834 (MC), half skein Black #8555 (CC)

16" (40cm) square pillow form

4 purchased decorator tassels

64" (163cm) upholstery or dressmakers cording 1/4" (6.5mm) diameter

Safety pin

*All pillows*

Size US 7 (4.5mm) needles

Tapestry needle

3 small frog closures for each pillow (optional)

*Lace trim (Beige pillow only)*
*Note*: Trim is worked sideways. With CC, CO 5 stitches. Work *Wrought Iron Lace* pattern until knitting measures 56" (142cm) from cast on edge, unstretched and unblocked, ending with row 4. BO.

*Wrought Iron Lace Chart*

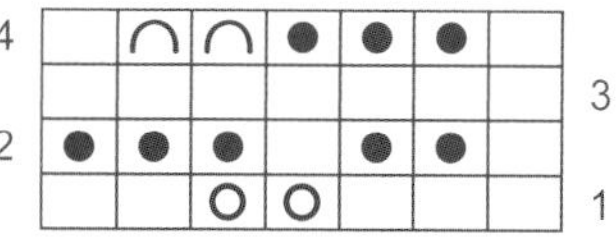


☐ RS: knit; WS: purl

⊡ yarnover

⊙ RS: purl; WS: knit

∩ bind off

*Braided I-cord trim (Blue pillow only; make 1 MC and 2 CC)*
With size US 7 (4.5mm) double pointed needles CO 3 stitches. Work I-cord for 80" (203cm). The trim consists of three lengths of I-cord braided together, one in MC and two in CC. The length of individual cords needed will vary depending on how tightly you braid the cords. To accommodate this, knit the cords to the recommended length, but don't bind off. Instead, transfer the stitches to a large safety pin as a stitch holder. Stitch the cast on edges of the three cords together. Pin to a corkboard, blocking board or other stationary object. Braid the three cords, checking braided length as you go, until you reach 64" (162cm). If your cords are too short, put the stitches back on a double pointed needle and continue knitting I-cord until you reach sufficient length. If the cords are too long, unravel until you reach the required length, place stitches back on the needle and BO. Stitch the bound off edges of the three cords together.

*I-cord trim (Rose pillow only)*
With size US 7 (4.5mm) double pointed needles and CC, CO 7 stitches. Work I-cord for 64" (162cm). BO. Attach a large safety pin to one end of the upholstery cording. Insert the pin and the cording into one open end of the I-cord. Thread the cotton cording through the knitted I-cord, using the safety pin to push the cotton cording through. When all the way through, remove the pin and using a short length of yarn and a tapestry needle, tack through the I-cord and cotton cording at each end to hold it in place.

## Finishing

*Beige pillow*
Block front to 12" (30cm) high by 16" (40cm) wide. Block backs to 9" (24cm) high by 16" (40cm) wide, but do not stretch or pin out the ribbing at the sides. Do not block *Wrought Iron Lace* trim. Using small amount of yellow worsted weight yarn and duplicate stitch, embroider the flame using photo as a guide. Pin straight selvedge stitch edge of lace trim to edge stitches of the pillow front, with the lace edge of the trim toward the center of the pillow. Pin pillow backs to the pillow front over the trim, right side to the inside, with cast on edges of the backs at top and bottom of pillow, catching the selvedge stitch of the trim between the front and backs. The backs will overlap to create an envelope opening to insert the pillow form. Backstitch all the way around the pillow. Turn pillow right side out.

*Blue pillow*
Block front to 18" (45cm) high by 14" (35cm) wide. Block backs to 14" (35cm) high by 14" (35cm) wide, but do not stretch or pin out the ribbing. Pin pillow backs to the pillow front over the trim, right side to the inside, with cast on edges of the backs at top and bottom of pillow. The backs will overlap to create an envelope opening to insert the pillow form. Backstitch all the way around the pillow. Turn pillow right side out. Starting at bottom center edge, whipstitch the braided trim along the outside seam, whipstitching the bind off and cast on edges of the I-cord to each other when they meet at bottom center.

*Rose pillow*
Block front to 16" (40cm) square. Block backs to 11" (28cm) high by 16" (40cm) wide, but do not stretch or pin out the ribbing. Pin pillow backs to the pillow front over the trim, right side to the inside, with cast on edges of the backs at top and bottom of pillow. The backs will overlap to create an envelope opening to insert the pillow form. Backstitch all the way around the pillow. Turn pillow right side out. Starting at lower center edge, whipstitch I-cord along outside pillow seam, whipstitching the bind off and cast on edges of the I-cord to each other when they meet. Sew one decorator tassel to each corner of pillow.

*All pillows*
Slip pillow form inside. If desired, sew 3 purchased frog closures at even intervals across the back opening.

Charleston's ornamental ironwork distinguishes the city from all others. It's hard to choose a favorite with so many fantastic, airy designs created from such a heavy material. I chose these three magnificent gates to inspire my pillow collection.

*Beige Pillow Chart*

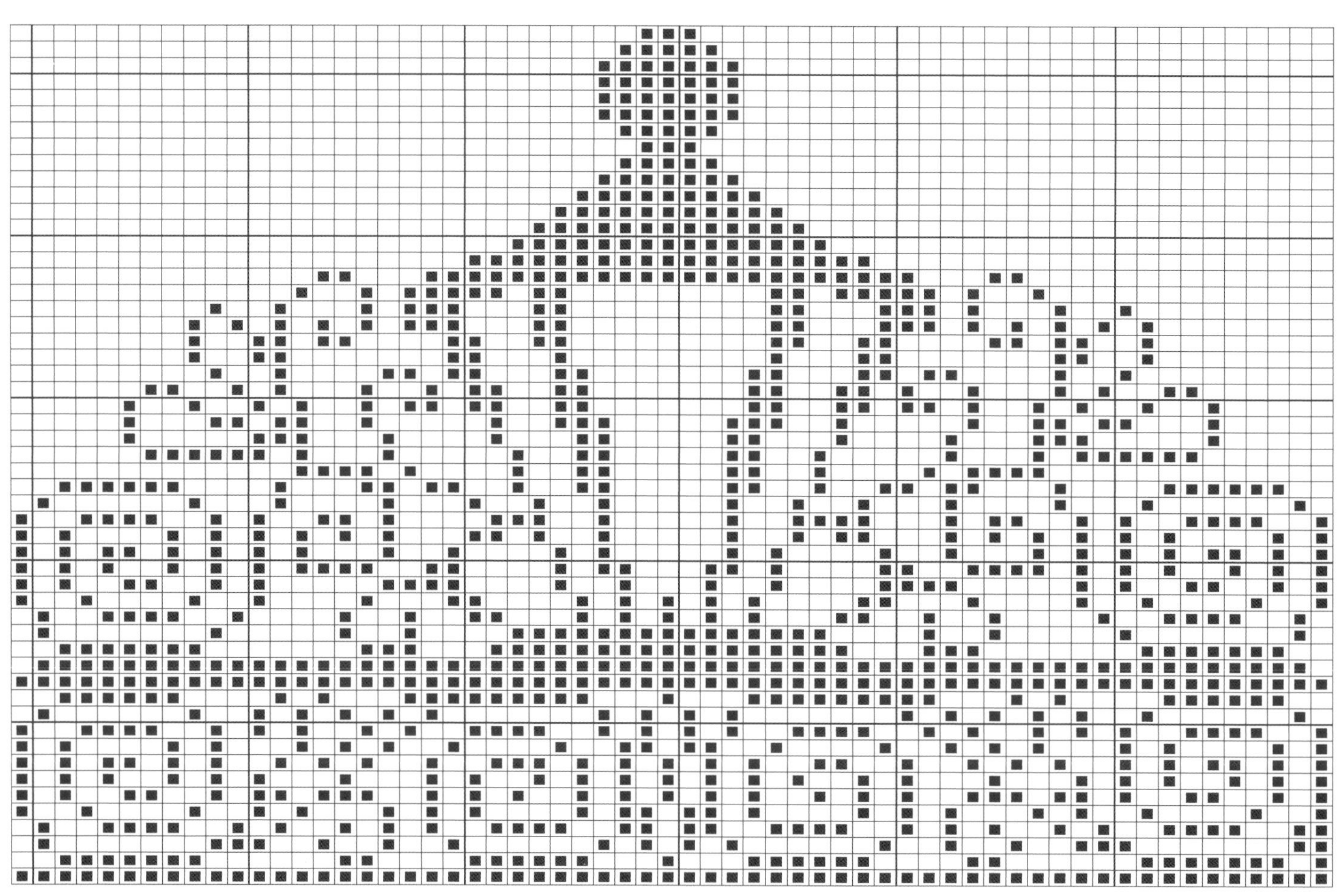

## Blue Pillow Chart

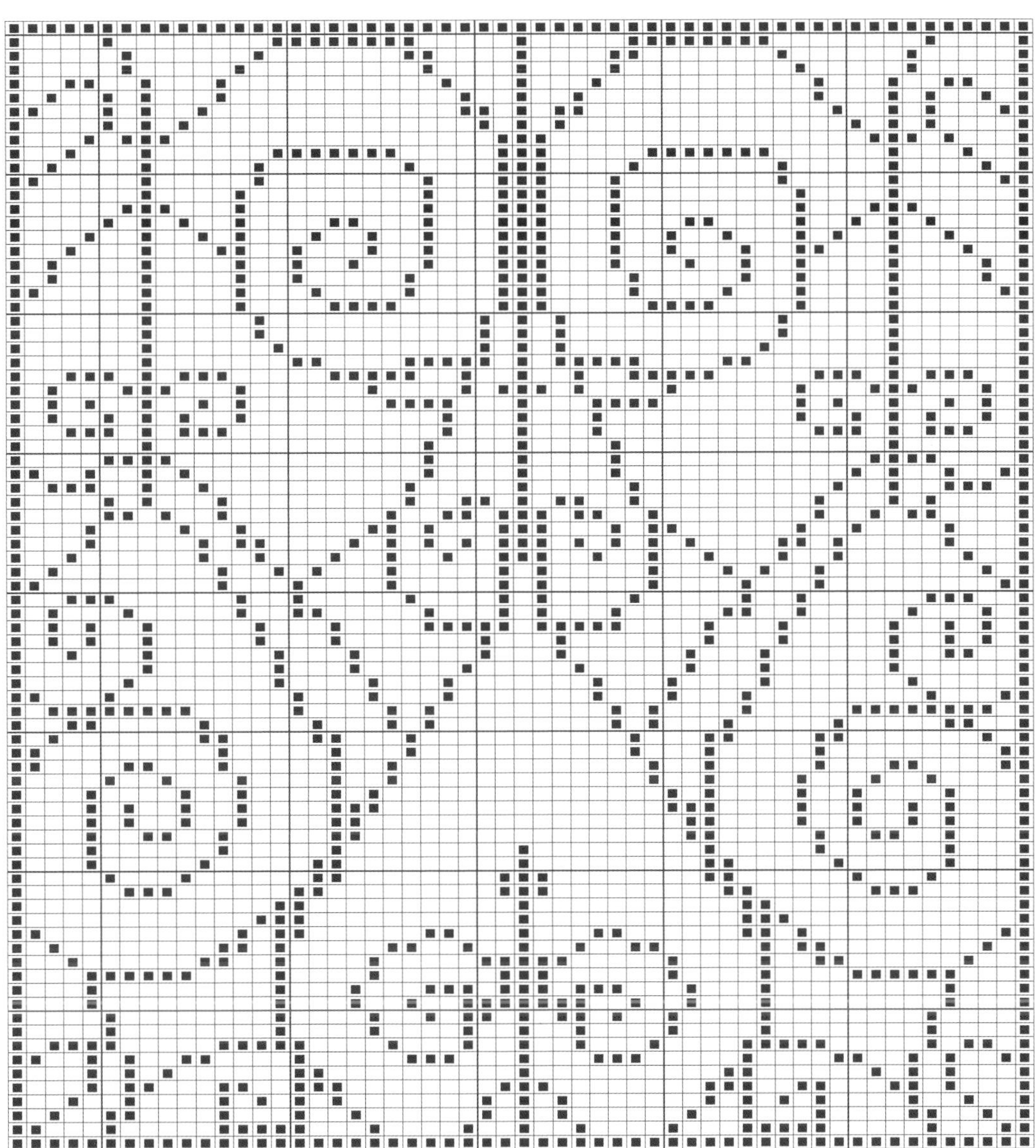

■ contrast color

## Rose Pillow Chart

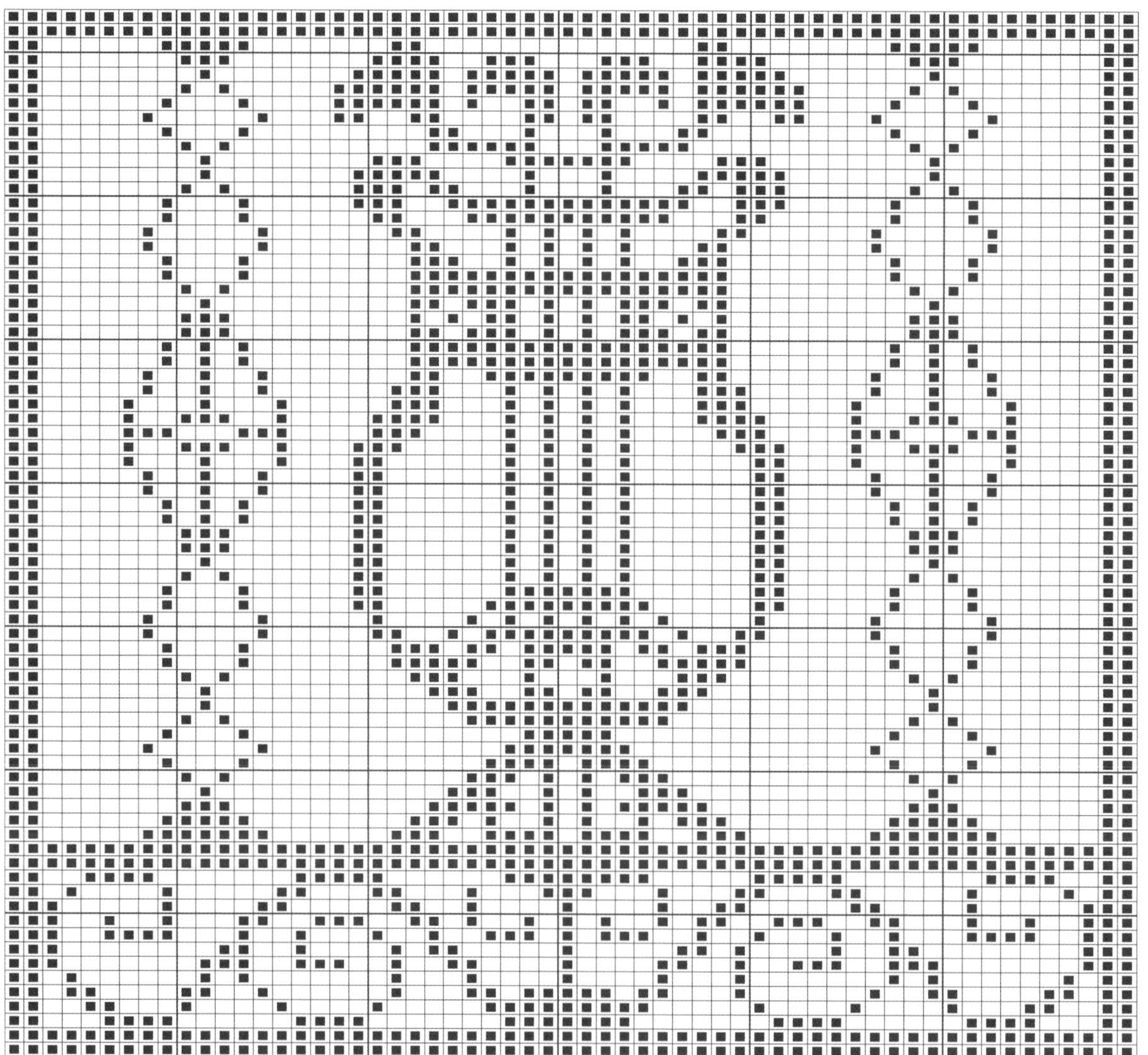

# Bourbon & Brown Sugar Pralines

*This sweet has all four of the Basic Southern Food Groups: brown sugar, butter, pecans, and bourbon. If you bring these to a party, you'll be the most popular person there, guaranteed. Make two or three times as many as you think you need— some for you to "taste test" and some to account for the number that will magically disappear in the middle of the night. I can't explain it. No one can. It just ... happens.*

## Directions

For best results, make one batch at a time. Preheat oven to 350 degrees. Put pecans in a single layer on an ungreased cookie sheet. Toast pecans lightly for 5-7 minutes, being careful not to burn. Allow to cool completely.

Butter sides of a heavy 2 quart saucepan. Add both sugars, half-and-half, and salt to saucepan. Cook over low heat, stirring constantly, until all the sugar is dissolved. Raise heat to medium and continue to cook, stirring constantly, until mixture boils. Reduce heat and stirring constantly, continue cooking to soft ball stage (a small amount of mixture dropped into chilled water forms a ball, but flattens when picked up with fingers) or 236-239 degrees on a candy thermometer. Depending on the quality of the pan, you may need to slowly increase heat to reach the desired temperature. Remove from heat.

*Tip*: Achieving the correct temperature is critical in candy-making. If you do not get the mixture hot enough, it will not set properly; too hot and it will be brittle. A candy thermometer is a good investment.

Add, but do not stir, butter, whiskey or bourbon and vanilla. The alcohol in the whiskey or bourbon will immediately bubble off. Cool for 5 minutes and then stir in toasted pecans. With a wooden spoon, beat mixture until the candy is no longer translucent and shiny and is thickened to the point that it will still drip slowly off the spoon, but isn't thin and watery, about 2-10 minutes, depending on how quickly your pan cools down. Working quickly before the mixture sets up in the pan, spoon by heaping tablespoons onto waxed paper or a Silpat® non-stick sheet. If the mixture begins to set up while still in the pan, do not return to heat. Rather, beat in a quarter teaspoon of very hot water and repeat until mixture is soft enough to drop from a spoon.

When completely cool, wrap individually in plastic wrap and store in an airtight container— if they last that long!

Makes about 16 3" pralines.

## Shopping List

1 cup granulated sugar

1 cup light brown sugar, packed

3/4 cup half-and-half

2 Tbl bourbon or whiskey (not extract)

1/4 tsp salt

2 Tbl butter, plus enough to butter pot

1 tsp pure vanilla extract

1 cup whole or coarsely broken pecans

Florida part of the Deep South? You might not think so if you've only been to Miami or Orlando on vacation. But in Jacksonville, Tallahassee, Lake City or any other point north of the I-4 corridor, you'll hear that slow, sweet drawl and be offered enough fried foods to clog every artery in your body. But even without the accent, Florida is Southern in *spirit*.

Florida's been my home for most of my life. Central Florida, to be precise, as there are really four Floridas. Central Florida, the corridor along I-4 and the Beach Line Expressway includes two of the world's most famous beaches (Daytona and Cocoa) on the east coast, winds past the Mouse House and all the nearby theme parks, and ends up on the west coast at Tampa/St. Pete, with the perennially award-winning Clearwater Beach and the Busch Gardens theme park. Got kids or grandkids? If you haven't been here yet, you will be.

North Florida (sometimes referred to as South Georgia or Lower Alabama) is definitely the most stereotypically Southern. Huge live oaks dripping Spanish moss, fish and hunting camps, cypress swamps and bayous, this is the Florida of hammocks tied between hundred year old trees.

Heading to the opposite end of the state, South Florida is the unlikely combination of staid "old money" and a lively, growing Caribbean and Latin community. South Beach with its Art Deco buildings and star-studded clubs and restaurants is *the* place to see and be seen for the beautiful people.

Last, but definitely not least, the Florida Keys. The country's southernmost spot, you can stand on one side of the street and watch the sun rise over the ocean, then turn around and wait awhile to watch the sun set into the ocean. Home to the only underwater national park in the U.S., the warm crystal clear waters are a snorkeling and diving paradise. Rent a bike to tour Key West, and at sunset head to Mallory Square for the daily sunset celebration.

Whichever of my Floridas you come to visit, thanks for stopping in and make sure you come back real soon!

# Treasure Coast Tennis Vest

Palm Beach, Florida

*Playground of the ultra-rich and famous, tennis is the game of choice in Palm Beach and tennis whites are de rigeur at the area's posh sporting clubs.*

*With no faults to be found, this beautifully textured and stylish vest from local designer* **Tanya Wade** *is an ace. Whether you're headed to the club to take on Serena and Venus, or just looking fab sipping cocktails in your favorite clubhouse, this vest has got you covered— game, set, match.*

## About this Project

**Skill Level:** Intermediate

**Finished Sizes:** S (M, L) to fit finished bust sizes 33½ (38½, 41½)" [85 (98, 105)cm]

**Fit Tip:** Semi-fitted. Choose a size 2-4" (5-10cm) larger than your actual bust measurement. Olivia is wearing a size Small.

**Project Gauge:** 20 stitches and 24 rows = 4" (10cm) in stockinette stitch on larger needles

## Shopping List

Blue Sky Alpaca *Skinny Dyed Cotton* (100% cotton, 150 yards/136m); 4 (5, 6) skeins Gardenia #311

Size US 6 (4mm) needles, straight or at least 24" (60cm) circular

Size US 4 (3.5mm) needle, 24" or 32" circular for armhole and neck trim

Stitch markers

Stitch holder

Tapestry needle

## Stitch Guide

*Make Bobble (mb)*
(K1, p1, k1, p1) in same stitch (4 stitches); turn, p4, turn, k4, turn, (p2tog) twice, turn and k2tog. (1 stitch)

*Oblique Rib*
Row 1 (RS): *K2, p2; repeat from * to end.
Row 2: *K1, p2, k1; repeat from * to end.
Row 3: *P2, k2; repeat from * to end.
Row 4: *P1, k2, p1; repeat from * to end.
Repeat rows 1-4, ending with row 4.

## Instructions

*Back*
With larger needles, CO 87 (97, 107) stitches.
Row 1 (WS): Knit.
Row 2: K3, *mb, k4; repeat from * across, ending mb, k3.
Work even in garter stitch for 4 rows.
Next row: Knit, decreasing 3 (1, 3) stitch(es) evenly across. [84 (96, 104) stitches]
Continue in stockinette stitch until piece measures 5 (5½, 6)" [13 (14, 15)cm]. Change to *Oblique Rib* pattern. Work in pattern until piece measures 9 (10, 11)" [23 (25, 28)cm] from cast on edge. Change to stockinette stitch and work even until piece measures 13 (13½, 14)" [33 (34.5, 36)cm] from cast on edge, ending with a wrong side row.
*Shape armholes*
BO 3 (4, 5) stitches at beginning of next 2 rows.
BO 2 (3, 3) stitches at beginning of next 2 rows.
Next (decrease) row (RS): K2, k2tog, knit to last 4 stitches, ssk, k2.
Working in stockinette stitch, repeat decrease row every 4th row a total of 5 times. [64 (72, 78) stitches].
Work even in stockinette stitch until armholes measures 6 (7, 7)" [17 (18, 18)cm].

*Shape shoulders and back neck*
BO 5 (6, 6) stitches at beginning of next 2 rows. Knit 11 (12, 14) stitches and turn, leaving remaining stitches on holder; work both sides separately.
Next row (WS): Purl 11 (12, 14) stitches. BO these 11 (12, 14) stitches.
With right side facing, rejoin yarn to remaining stitches. From holder, BO center 32 (36, 38) stitches, knit to end.
Next row: Purl 11 (12, 14) stitches. BO these 11 (12, 14) stitches.

*Front*
Work as for back to 8 rows less than back to beginning of armhole shaping, ending with a wrong side row.
*Shape neck*
*Note:* Leave center 2 stitches on holder for size small only. These will be worked when you do the trim.
Next row (RS): K41 (48, 52) stitches, turn, leaving remaining stitches on holder.
Work each side separately.
Next row: Purl.
Next (decrease) row (RS): Knit to last 4 stitches, ssk, k2.
Next row: Purl.
Decrease 1 stitch at neck edge as set on next and 2 following RS rows. [37 (44, 48) stitches].
Next row: Purl. Piece now measures same as back to start of armhole shaping.
*Shape armhole and neck*
Next row (RS): BO 3 (4, 5) stitches, knit to last 4 stitches, ssk, k2.
Next row: Purl.
Next row: BO 2 (3, 3) stitches, knit to end. [31 (36, 39) stitches]
Next row: Purl.
Next (decrease) row (RS): K2, k2tog, knit to last 4 stitches, ssk, k2.
Next row: Purl to last 4 stitches, p2tog, p2.
Next row: K2, k2tog, knit to end.
Next row: Purl.
Continue to decrease one stitch at armhole edge on next row and every right side row twice more, and decrease one stitch at neck edge on next row and every following 4th row until 16 (18, 20) stitches remain. Work even until armhole measures 6¾ (7, 7)" [17 (18, 18)cm], ending with a WS row.
*Shape shoulder*
BO 5 (6, 6) stitches at beginning of next row.
Next row: Work even.
BO remaining 11 (12, 14) stitches.
With right side facing, rejoin yarn to stitches from holder, complete to match first side, reversing shaping.

## Finishing

Block front and back according to chart on page 153. Sew right shoulder seam.

*Neck edging*
With RS facing and smaller needle, pick up and knit 134 (138, 138) stitches around the neck opening, picking up the two held stitches for size small as you work. Mark center front of v-neck.
Next row: Knit.
Next row: Knit to 2 stitches before marker, ssk, k2tog, knit to end.
BO all stitches kwise.

*Armhole edging*
With RS facing and smaller needle, pick up and knit 92 (96, 96) stitches evenly around armhole.
Next 2 rows: Knit.
BO all stitches kwise.

Sew left shoulder seam. Repeat armhole edging. Sew side seams (seaming the open edge of armhole edging as well) using mattress stitch. Weave in ends.

Palm Beach is still the winter home of the old-money rich, but it's also home to world champion tennis stars. In addition to Venus and Serena, Chris Evert and Andy Roddick also call the area "home." Evert's Tennis Academy is in nearby Boca Raton.

## Florida's Best Beaches

Nestled between the Atlantic and the Gulf of Mexico, most Floridians can reach a great beach within an hour. Year after year, Florida's beaches populate every top 10 list of the country's best. Whether you want to ride the biggest waves on the East Coast or snorkel and float in the smooth warm waters of the Gulf, Florida has the perfect beach for your vacation. Here are some perennial favorites:

*Siesta Beach*, Siesta Key - A beautiful crescent shaped beach on the Gulf of Mexico, Siesta Beach has powdery white sand made of nearly pure quartz crystal. You can snorkel and scuba dive the coral rocks and caves right off the beach, the turquoise waters are so clean and clear. More information is available online at SiestaKeyChamber.com.

*Fort DeSoto Park*, St. Petersburg - This park consists of five interconnected islands (keys), totaling 1,136 acres. In addition to miles of perfect sandy beaches, the islands are home to more than 290 species of birds and a variety of ecosystems. The historic fort, built as a coastal citadel during the Spanish-American war, is on the National Register of Historic Places. There are two piers, picnic spots, boat launches, and numerous camping areas. You can find more information at PinellasCounty.org.

*Fernandina Beach*, Amelia Island - Just off the coast of Jacksonville, Amelia Island has one of the most unspoiled stretches of coastline in Florida. Thirteen miles long and four miles wide, it's not hard at all to find a patch of sand you can have all to yourself. Fernandina Beach, the island's main town, is known as the "Isle of Eight Flags," owing to the various nations and marauding pirates that have at one time or another ruled the island from historic Fort San Carlos, built by Spanish settlers in 1686. The island was once an important seaport, attracting wealthy shippers and merchants. Today, its 50 square block downtown is on the National Register of Historic Places. The entire district is like a Victorian village, with stately gingerbread-covered houses, many of them now B&B's. Excellent seafood restaurants and great shopping help make Amelia Island a perfect getaway spot.

*Andrews State Park*, Panama City - The 1,260 acre park with 1.5 miles of sugary, white sand beaches has won more awards than you can shake a bikini at. The park has everything you could need for an outdoor vacation with hiking trails, fishing jetties, campgrounds and a swimming lagoon. Panama City is a sport fishing mecca and scuba divers have plenty to explore in this "Wreck Capital of the South." More information can be found at VisitPanamaCityBeach.com.

# Beachcomber Lariat Set

Key Largo, Florida

*Florida's extraordinary coastline, bedecked with its own delicate necklace of seafoam washed gently ashore during high tide, depositing treasures among the foam, is the inspiration for the Beachcomber Lariat and Charm Bracelet. The undulating texture of the soft cotton yarn and the shifting pattern created by different length drop stitches evoke the ripples left in the sand as the tide retreats. The sea glass, shells, pottery shard and driftwood "beads" can be purchased or taken from your own collection of beach treasures. Knit it wider for a shawl, or keep it skinny and wrap, wrap, wrap it to decorate your own lovely neck. The matching bracelet shows off your beach treasure collection and tinkles gently as you move. Perfect for when you're stuck in the snow, but dreaming of the tropics.*

## About this Project

**Skill Level:** Easy

**Finished Sizes:** Lariat is approximately 3" wide by 92" long (7cm x 2.3m), including fringe. The bracelet is sized for S/M (L/XL) wrist and finished size is 7 (8)" [18 (20)cm].

**Project Gauge:** 16 stitches = 3" (7cm) and 8 rows = 2" (5cm) in *Low Tide Stitch*

*Note:* Gauge is not critical but will impact the finished size and the amount of yarn used.

## Shopping List

Cascade *Ultra Pima* (100% cotton, 220 yards/200m); 1 skein Ecru #3718 for bracelet and lariat

Size US 7 (4.5mm) needles

Sea glass, shell and driftwood beads (Etsy.com)

Beading needle

Tapestry needle

Small crochet hook to apply fringe

6½ (7½)" [17 (19)cm] length of bracelet chain

One bracelet closure

Two jump rings

Matching thread and sewing needle

## Stitch Guide

*Abbreviations*
Kw2: Knit, wrapping yarn around needle twice
Kw3: Knit, wrapping yarn around needle three times

*Low Tide Stitch*
Row 1 (RS): Sl1 pwise wyib, k1, *kw2, kw3, kw2, k3; repeat from * to last two stitches, k2.
Row 2: Sl1 pwise wyib, knit to end, dropping extra wraps.
Row 3: Sl1 pwise wyib, knit to end.
Row 4: Sl1 pwise wyib, knit to end.
Row 5: Sl1 pwise wyib, k4, *kw2, kw3, kw2, k3; repeat from *, ending last repeat with k2.
Row 6: Sl1 pwise wyib, knit to end, dropping extra wraps.
Row 7: Sl1 pwise wyib, knit to end.
Row 8: Sl1 pwise wyib, knit to end.

## Instructions

### Lariat

CO 16 stitches.
Row 1 and 2: Sl1 pwise wyif, knit to end.
Row 3-6: Work 4 rows of *Low Tide Stitch*.
Repeat row 3-6 until piece measures 72" (182cm).
Repeat row 1-2. BO all stitches. Weave in the ends before applying trim.

*Treasure Net trim*
Cut 9 strands of yarn 40" (1.1m) long. Fold each strand in half and apply 9 strands as fringe evenly spaced along each short end, making sure to place fringe in first and last stitches. Tie fringe into fishnet, using the chart for directions and tying a bead or shell into the knots as desired. The lariat shown has 18 beads or shells on each end. Cut 18 strands of yarn 12" (30cm) long.

Using two strands held together, apply fringe to each of the nine bottom knots of the fishnet. Cut the ends evenly across at 4" (10cm) creating a 6 strand tassel at each knot.

## Bracelet

String 36 (42) shells, beads, and glass pieces onto yarn. CO 7 stitches.
Row 1: Knit.
Row 2: Using knitted cast on, CO 4 stitches. Place bead. BO 4 stitches. Knit to end.
Repeat row 2 until piece measures $6^1/_2$ ($7^1/_2$)" [17 (19)cm]. BO all stitches. Weave in ends before applying chain.

Using jump rings, attach bracelet clasp to the bracelet chain. Lay knitted bracelet flat. Place chain on top, lining top edge of bracelet chain two stitches down from the top edge of knitting. Whipstitch the top edge of bracelet chain to knitting. Fold knitting over chain and whipstitch through all layers and the bottom edge of the chain, creating two tiers of charms.

*Low Tide Stitch Chart*

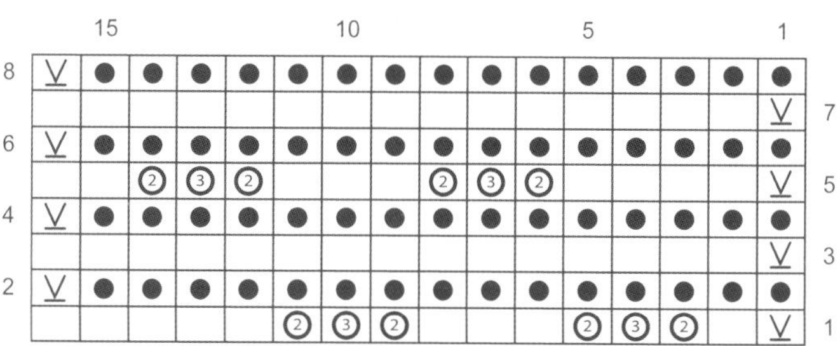


RS and WS: slip stitch as if to purl, with yarn in back

RS: knit stitch

RS: knit, wrapping yarn twice around needle

RS: knit, wrapping yarn three times around needle

WS: knit stitch, dropping any extra wraps

*Treasure Net Trim*

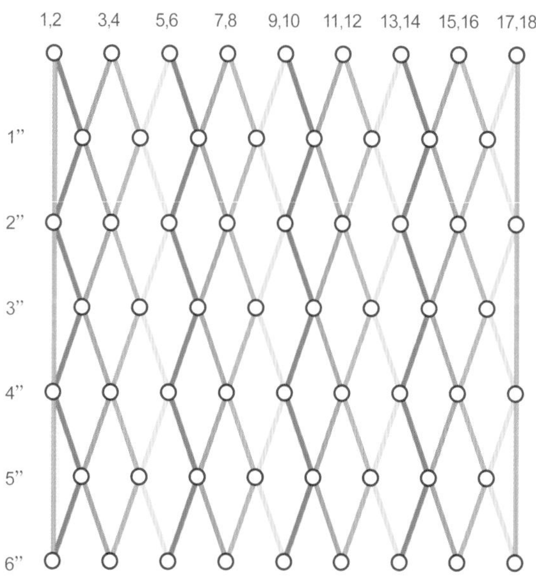

- Sometimes more is just more. Don't use too many beads on the Treasure Net trim of the lariat or it will become overly heavy.
- You can place a tiny bead of flexible fabric glue on each of the knots in the Treasure Net trim for extra hold, if desired.
- To make tying the fishnet evenly as easy as a walk on the beach, pin the end of the lariat to a blocking board and use the printed grid. Don't have a blocking board? Tack it to a board (or wall?) over a piece of graph paper marked off in 1" (2.5cm) increments.

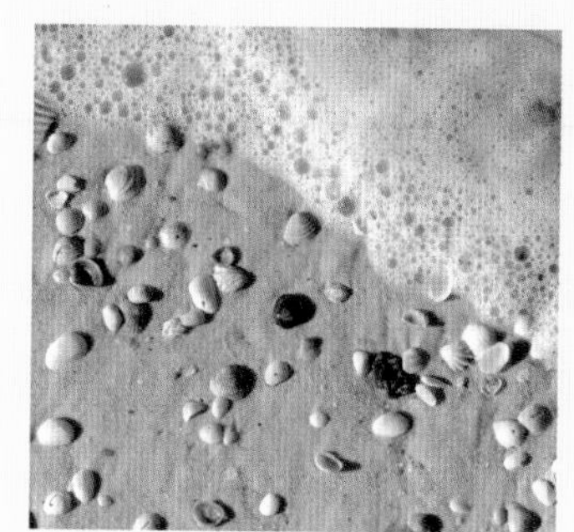

Growing up in Cocoa Beach, one of my favorite things to do was to comb the high tide line for "treasures." When my son was little, I'd accompany him on similar hunts. Someday, maybe with my grandchildren (hint, hint)?

# Sunset Moebius

Sanibel Island, Florida

*This lacy summer scarf was inspired by the stunning orange and gold sunsets that are the only good part of the hottest, stickiest summer days in Florida. The touches of gold and the sparkle of the glass beads are reminiscent of the glint of the setting sun on the surface of the calm seas of Florida's beautiful Gulf Coast. It can be worn simply around the neck like a bit of knitted jewelry, down on the shoulders as a light wrap or doubled around your neck as lightweight filler for blouses or jackets. Wear it and dream of tropical sunsets, ice cold fruity drinks and tall, well-oiled men fanning you with palm fronds.*

## About this Project

**Skill Level:** Intermediate

**Finished Size:** Approximately 50" (127cm) in circumference by 5½" (14cm) wide

**Project Gauge:** Gauge is not critical to this piece. If you knit tightly, go up one or two needle sizes. The fabric should be very open and light.

## Shopping List

Argosy Luxury Yarns *Haiku 2 Ply* (55% silk, 45% cashmere, 200 yards/183m); 1 skein Tortilla Soup (MC)

Artyarns *Beaded Mohair & Sequins* (80% silk with glass beads and sequins, 20% mohair, 114 yards/104m); 1 skein Gold/ Beige #164G (CC)

Size US 7 (4.5mm) 40-48" (100-120cm) circular needle

Stitch marker

Tapestry needle

120 size 6/0 glass beads to complement MC

Beading needle

## Stitch Guide

*Drop Stitch Inset*
Round 1: *K1, yo; repeat from * to end.
Round 2: Knit all knit stitches, dropping all yarnovers off the needle without working them.

*Beaded Picot Bind Off*
BO 3 stitches. *Move the stitch on the right needle to the left needle. Using knitted cast on method, CO 3 stitches. Move bead to place it against the left needle. BO 8 stitches loosely, capturing the bead in the first stitch of the bind off. Repeat from * until only one stitch remains. Break yarn leaving 6" (15cm) tail. Draw tail through remaining stitch.

## Instructions

Using MC and Moebius Cast On, CO 240 stitches. Place marker to mark beginning of round. Join.
Round 1 and 2: Using MC, knit two rounds.
Round 3 and 4: Purl.
Round 5 and 6: Knit. Cut yarn and change to CC.
Round 7 and 8: Purl.
Round 9 and 10: Knit.
Round 11 and 12: Purl. Cut yarn and change to MC.
Round 13: Knit.
Round 14 and 15: Work the two rounds of the *Drop Stitch Inset.*
Round 16: Knit. Cut yarn and change to CC.
Round 17 and 18: Purl.
Round 19 and 20: Knit.
Round 21: Purl.
Round 22: Purl. Cut yarn. String MC with 120 glass beads.
Round 23: With MC, knit. Pushing glass beads down yarn until needed for bind off.
Round 24: Remove stitch marker and BO all stitches in MC using *Beaded Picot Bind Off.*

## Finishing

Block moebius lightly, pinning out the picots. You may find it easier to block one section at a time, slipping the moebius over the narrow end of an ironing board to block. Weave in ends.

## Florida's Latin Heritage

Modern-day Miami is known for its distinct Latin beat, but Florida's Latin heritage is centuries old. There's no denying Florida's deep Latin roots, with historic forts and missions left as reminders of 16th century conquistadors and clerics, 19th century Cuban cigar factories and 20th century treasure-hunters searching for lost Spanish gold.

*St. Augustine* – Spanish explorer Ponce de Leon arrived on St. Augustine's shore in 1513, naming the land "Florida" (the land of flowers). 52 years later, Pedro Menendez de Aviles founded St. Augustine, the U.S.'s oldest European settlement. The city's waterfront is dominated by Castillo de San Marco, a coquina limestone fortification and the only remaining 17th century fort in the country. Historic St. George Street and its environs are filled with shops and restaurants. I recommend the 1905 salad and *ropa vieja* at the landmark Columbia Restaurant! Adjacent to St. George Street is the Colonial Spanish Quarter, a living history museum comprised of 10 buildings where costumed interpreters give visitors a glimpse into the lives of a mid-18th century blacksmith, carpenter, leatherworker, candlemaker and soldier's wife. Other sites include the fantastic Spanish-influenced architecture of Flagler College, originally a hotel built in the late 19th century by magnate Henry Flagler; the old mission *Nombre de Dios* (Name of God) on the site of the first Catholic Mass spoken in the New World (in 1565); the Fountain of Youth; the oldest European schoolhouse in the U.S.; and the Lightener Museum, housed in yet another Henry Flagler hotel.

*Tampa* – Come to the Gulf Coast for the fabulous beaches, but while you're here, don't miss Ybor City, a National Historic Landmark District near downtown Tampa. This neighborhood sprang up in the 19th century to serve the Cuban immigrants working in Vincente Martinez-Ybor's cigar factories. One hundred fifty years later, it's one of Florida's hottest nightclub spots. The district still has plenty to offer before the sun goes down— stroll the streets, people-watch, drink thick Cuban coffee, eat your way from bakery to bakery, and visit the Ybor City Museum State Park, featuring restored *casitas*, originally built to house the factory workers and their families.

*Key West* – If it's Spanish gold you seek, head to Mel Fisher's Maritime Museum. The museum displays gold, silver and gems recovered by Fisher and his band of treasure hunters as a result of their sixteen year quest to locate the remains of eight wrecked ships from the Tierra Firma flota, sunk during a hurricane in 1622 while crossing the Florida Straits. The museum also exhibits a variety of artifacts that paint a picture of Spanish military and naval life in the 17th century.

# Fried Sweet Plantains

*Fried sweet plantains can be served as a side dish as a nice counter-point to spicier entrees, by themselves as a sweet treat, or as a topping for ice cream for something truly decadent. Plantains are a starchier version of bananas. For this dish, wait until the plantain skins are almost-black to fully-black. That's when they'll be soft and delectably sweet. Make more than you think you'll need— it's not likely you'll have leftovers.*

## Directions

Peel plantains. Slice on the diagonal in 2" slices or cut in half and then in quarters lengthwise. Put brown sugar in a small plastic food bag. Drop a few pieces of sliced plantain in the bag at a time and shake to lightly coat.

Heat oil and butter together in a large pan on medium high heat until it starts to sizzle. Place slices in a single layer in the pan. Cook about 2 minutes until lightly caramelized. Turn and cook second side for approximately two minutes. Remove from pan. Do not drain on paper towels. Serve immediately.

Serves 8.

### Shopping List

4 Tbl salted butter

1/2 cup cooking oil

4 very ripe plantains

1/2 cup light brown sugar

The largest state east of the Mississippi, Georgia is remarkably diverse. From Atlanta to the Blue Ridge mountains, to genteel Savannah to the wild barrier islands, a vacation in Georgia is one you'll never forget.

Scarlett O'Hara's Atlanta burned almost completely to the ground in 1864, and has been replaced by a modern metropolitan city, the self-proclaimed "capital of the South." Despite the destruction, Atlanta has managed to retain its very Southern roots through the rebuilding.

One of my favorite places to see Old Atlanta is Underground Atlanta. Six blocks long, the area was ground level prior to the building of viaducts one level overhead in the 1920's to help ease traffic. For the next 40 years, the old storefronts were used for storage as the shops moved to their second floors— the new street level.

In the late 1960's, Underground Atlanta was placed on the National Register of Historic Places and developed as a retail and entertainment center. It closed for most of 1980's and was finally re-opened in 1989 after massive refurbishment. Take the guided tour to get a taste of Atlanta history from the Civil War through the Civil Rights movement.

On the coast, Savannah is the perfect spot for a romantic weekend getaway. Many of the historic mansions are now inns, so choose one and then just park the car. Savannah is best appreciated on foot, wandering from square to square (there are 21 of them), strolling through the parks, and peeking into private gardens along the way. Because all that walking is bound to build up an appetite, head to the waterfront along historic River Street. The restored cotton warehouses are now home to fabulous eateries, where you can indulge in some of the best Southern cuisine.

From Savannah, you're just a hop, skip and a jump to the barrier islands. Sunbathe on Tybee Island's wide beach, or tie up those hiking boots and head to one of the completely undeveloped islands to commune with nature. Or do both?

Wherever your visit to Georgia takes you, I know that like an old sweet song, Georgia will be on your mind.

# *Lighthouse Tunic*

Tybee Island, Georgia

*If you are planning a visit to historic and beautiful Savannah, don't forget to pack your swimsuit for a jaunt to Tybee Island. One of the lesser-known gems of the Atlantic beaches, this tiny barrier island just 18 miles from Savannah boasts a three mile stretch of wide, flat, pristine white sand. Since 1773, the Tybee Island Lighthouse, painted in an eye-popping graphic stripe, has been standing guard over the island.*

*The lighthouse inspired this body-skimming tunic, great to wear over a pair of white capris, shorts or your bathing suit. The swing-away design and color-blocking are a nod to the lighthouse's shape and stripes. Its mid-thigh length and soft drape will flatter a wide range of body shapes and sizes. Wear it over a tank for a layered look, or wear it alone to show your tan off to its best advantage. Either way, you may need some guarding of your own!*

## About this Project

**Skill Level:** Easy

**Finished Sizes:** Finished bust sizes 34 (36, 39½, 42½)" [86, (91, 100, 108)cm]

**Fit Tip:** Designed with 0-2" (0-5cm) of ease at the bust. Please choose a size accordingly. Elisha is wearing the smallest size.

**Project Gauge:** 15 stitches and 22 rows = 4" (10cm) in stockinette stitch on larger needle

## Stitch Guide

*4x4 Rib (in the round)*
All rounds: *K4, p4; repeat from * to end.

## Instructions

*Note:* Back and front are worked in the round to the armholes.

*Body*
With Bleached and larger needle, CO 176 (184, 192, 208) stitches, placing marker after stitch 88 (92, 96, 104) and another to mark beginning of round. Join. Work 8 rounds of *4x4 Rib*. Work evenly in stockinette stitch for 14 (16, 19, 10) rounds, decreasing 4 (4, 0, 0) stitches evenly in the 4th round. [172 (180, 192, 208) stitches].
*Body decrease round*: *K2tog, knit to 2 stitches before the marker, ssk, slip marker; repeat from * to end of round. (4 stitches decreased).
Repeat *body decrease round* 9 (9, 7, 10) times every 10 rounds, then 1 (1, 3, 1) time(s) every 5 rounds, for a total of 11 (11, 11, 12) decrease rounds. [128 (136, 148, 160) stitches].
Work even for 5 (4, 12, 4) rounds. A total of 122 (124, 125, 128) total rounds have been worked.
At this point, divide for front and back as explained below.
**At the same time**, after a total of 90 (94, 96, 98) rounds, change to Azalea until round 135 (137, 140, 142) is completed (approximately 2" [5cm] after dividing front and back). Then change back to Bleached for remainder of garment. See *Tips* below for color change technique in the round.
*Divide for front and back*
Knit the first stitch of the next round to move working yarn to proper location. Slip worked stitch back to left needle. Move the previous 64 (68, 74, 80) stitches to a stitch holder or spare needle/cable to be worked later for front. Work remaining 64 (68, 74, 80) stitches back and forth for back as follows.

*Back*
*Armhole shaping*
BO 3 (3, 4, 4) stitches at beginning of each of the next 2 rows.
[58 (62, 66, 72) stitches]. Then BO 1 (2, 3, 3) stitches at the beginning of each of the next 2 rows. [56 (58, 60, 66) stitches].

## Shopping List

Rowan *All Seasons Cotton* (60% cotton, 40% acrylic, 98 yards/90m); 7 (8, 8, 9) skeins Bleached #182 and 2 (2, 3, 3) skeins Gladioli #238

Size US 9 (5.5mm) 24" (60cm) circular needle

Size US 7 (4.5mm) 16" (40cm) circular needle

Stitch markers

Stitch holder

Tapestry needle

*Armhole decrease row (worked on RS)*: K1, ssk, knit to last 3 stitches, k2tog, k1.
Repeat *armhole decrease row* on every RS row 5 (4, 5, 6) times, then on every other RS row 1 (1, 1, 1) time, then every 3rd RS row 1 (0, 2, 1) time(s), then every 5th RS row 1 (3, 1, 2) time(s).
Work even for 9 (5, 11, 7) rows, ending with a WS row. [166 (174, 176, 182) total rows/rounds worked and 38 (40, 40, 44) stitches remain].
*Dividing for back neck and shoulders*
Next row (RS): K17 (17, 17, 18). BO 4 (6, 6, 8). K17 (17, 17, 18). [34 (34, 34, 36) stitches remain; 17 (17, 17, 18) stitches per shoulder].
*Back left shoulder shaping*
Row 1 (WS): Purl to last 3 stitches, p3tog, decreasing 2 stitches at neck edge. [15 (15, 15, 16) stitches]
Row 2 (RS): BO 5 (4, 3, 3) stitches at neck edge, knit to end. [10 (11, 12, 13) stitches]
Row 3: Purl to last 2 stitches, p2tog (decreasing 1 stitch at neck edge). [9 (10, 11, 12) stitches]
Row 4: Ssk, knit to last 2 stitches, k2tog (decreasing 1 stitch each at both neck and armhole edge). [7 (8, 9, 10) stitches]
Row 5: Purl to last 2 stitches, p2tog (decreasing 1 stitch at neck edge).
BO remaining 6 (7, 8, 9) stitches.
Join ball of yarn to back right neck edge, prepared to knit WS row.
*Back right shoulder shaping*
Row 1 (WS): BO 5 (4, 3, 3) stitches at neck edge, purl to end. [12 (13, 14, 15) stitches]
Row 2 (RS): Knit to last 3 stitches, k3tog, decreasing 2 stitches at neck edge. [10 (11, 12, 13) stitches]
Row 3: P2tog, purl to end (decreasing 1 neck edge stitch). [9 (10, 11, 12) stitches]

One of the few 18th century lighthouses still operating, the Tybee Lighthouse has survived earthquakes, hurricanes Civil War and being moved more than 50 yards. The graphic black and white stripe design dates to 1916. The lens magnifies its 1000 watt light bulb so it's visible for 18 miles!

Row 4: Ssk, knit to last 2 stitches, k2tog (decreasing 1 stitch each at both neck and armhole edge). [7 (8, 9, 10) stitches]
Row 5: P2tog (decreasing 1 stitch at neck edge), purl to end.
Row 6: BO remaining 6 (7, 8, 9) stitches.
Place remaining stitches held for front on needle. Attach yarn to front, prepared to knit RS row.

*Front*
*Armhole shaping*
BO 3 (3, 4, 4) stitches at beginning of each of the next 2 rows. [58 (62, 66, 72) stitches].
Then BO 2 (2, 2, 3) stitches at the beginning of each of the next 2 rows. [54 (58, 62, 66) stitches].
*Armhole decrease row (worked on RS)*: K1, ssk, knit to last 3 stitches, k2tog, k1.
Repeat *armhole decrease row* on every RS row 4 (5, 6, 7) times. Purl 1 row. [134 (140, 142, 148) total rows/rounds worked and 44 (46, 48, 50) stitches remain].
*Dividing for front neck and shoulders*
Next row (RS): K17 (18, 19, 20). BO 10 (10, 10, 10). K17 (18, 19, 20). [34 (36, 38, 40) stitches remain; 17 (18, 19, 20) per shoulder].
*Front right shoulder shaping*
Purl 1 row to neck edge.
*Front right decrease row (worked on RS)*: K1, ssk, knit to last 3 stitches, k2tog, k1.
Repeat *front right decrease row* every other RS row 2 (2, 3, 3) time(s), then every 5th RS row 2 (2, 1, 1) time(s). Work even for 1 (3, 7, 5) row(s). [168 (170, 174, 178) rows/rounds worked and 7 (8, 9, 10) stitches remain].
*Neck edge decrease row (worked on RS)*: K1, ssk, knit to end (1 stitch decreased at neck edge).
Work even for 5 (9, 8, 10) rows. [174 (180, 183, 189) rows/ rounds have been worked].
BO remaining 6 (7, 8, 9) stitches.
Join ball of yarn to front left neck edge, prepared to knit WS row. Purl 1 row.
*Front left shoulder shaping*
*Front left decrease row (worked on RS)*: K1, ssk, knit to last 3 stitches, k2tog, k1.
Repeat *front left decrease row* every other RS row 2 (2, 3, 3) times, then every 5th RS row 2 (2, 1, 1) time(s). Work even for 1 (3, 7, 5) row(s). [168 (170, 174, 178) rows/rounds worked and 7 (8, 9, 10) stitches remain].
*Neck edge decrease row (worked on RS)*: Knit to last 3 stitches, ssk, k1 (1 stitch decreased at neck edge).
Work even for 5 (9, 8, 10) rows. BO remaining 6 (7, 8, 9) stitches.

## Finishing

Stitch shoulder seams.

*Armhole band*
With Bleached and smaller needle, starting at bottom of armhole, pick up and knit every stitch evenly around armhole. Place marker and join for working in the round.
Round 1: K1, p1, k2tog, p1; repeat from * to end, replacing the last k2tog with a knit stitch if necessary to finish with a purl stitch.
Round 2: K1, p1; repeat from * to end.
Rounds 3-8: Repeat round 2.
BO in rib.
Repeat for second armhole.

*Neck band*
With Bleached and smaller needle, starting at center back, pick up and knit every stitch evenly around neckline. Place marker and join for working in the round.
Round 1: K1, p1, k2tog, p1; repeat from * to end, replacing the last k2tog with a knit stitch if necessary to finish with a purl stitch.
Round 2: K1, p1; repeat from * to end.
Rounds 3-12: Repeat round 2.
BO in rib.
Weave in all ends. Block according to chart on page 152.

## Tips

- Since the striped section is knit in the round, use this "jogless stripe" technique to minimize the jog when changing colors: After the last stitch of the round where the color changes, pull the stitch (old color) from below the first stitch of the round just completed up to the left hand needle. Knit the lifted stitch (old color) together with the first stitch of the round (new color). A video of this technique is available on PlanetPurl.com.

- For a lower cut front, simply make the neck band narrower by 4 rows. You can reduce it by 6 rows, but if you do, reduce the armhole bands by 2 rows as well for better visual balance.

### Georgia's Barrier Islands

Georgia's modest 100 miles of coastline (as the crow flies) is dotted with 17 barrier islands just off shore. A haven for pirates and later the private playgrounds for the super-rich, the islands provide a unique view of nature almost untouched by human hands. Here are some highlghts:

*Cumberland Island* - Only 300 visitors a day are permitted on the island, and all arrive by Park Service boat.

*Jekyll Island* - Membership in the exclusive Jekyll Island Club included names like Rockefeller, Vanderbilt, Morgan and Pulitzer.

*St. Simon's Island* - Once the home of rice and cotton plantations, the island has become a mecca for artists.

# "Frankly My Dear" Fichu

Atlanta, Georgia

*A certain fictional Southern heroine was ahead of her time—"reduce, reuse, recycle" never looked so good as when she used her green velvet drapes, gold trim and tassels to make a fancy dress. Scarlett needed something stunning to wear to convince a charming scalawag to give her money to save her plantation after those nasty carpetbaggers raised her taxes.*

*Perfect for cool summer evenings or as a modest cover for bare shoulders at a summer wedding, this lacy fichu was inspired by that most famous drapery dress. Knit in a classic feather and fan pattern, its linen fabric is much lighter than velvet drapes but equally fetching as a frame for your own pretty neck and shoulders. With a simple 4 row repeat and only one row of increases and decreases, why fiddle-dee-dee, it's quite an easy lace knitting project, even if you've never knit lace before!*

## *About this Project*

**Skill Level:** Intermediate

**Finished Sizes:** Sized for S/M (L/XL) with finished sizes of 8" (20cm) high x 17 (21)" (43 [53]cm) long at neck edge (not including ties and tassels)

**Project Gauge:** 18 stitches x 20 rows = 4" (10cm) in *Scarlett's Feather and Fan* after blocking

## *Stitch Guide*

*Scarlett's Feather and Fan (worked in multiples of 18 plus 6)*
Row 1 (RS): Sl1 kwise wyib, knit to last stitch, p1.
Row 2: Sl1 kwise wyib, k2, purl to last 3 stitches, k2, p1.
Row 3: Sl1 kwise wyib, k2, *[k2tog] three times, [yo, k1] six times, [k2tog] three times; repeat from * to last three stitches, k2, p1.
Row 4: Sl1 kwise wyib, knit to last stitch, p1.
Repeat rows 1-4 until desired length.

## *Instructions*

*Yellow ruffle edge*
With Yellow, CO 168 (195) stitches loosely and evenly.
Row 1 (RS): Sl1 kwise wyib, knit to last stitch, p1.
Row 2: Sl1 kwise wyib, knit to last stitch, p1.
Row 3: Same as Row 1.
Row 4: Sl1 kwise wyib, k2, purl to last 3 stitches, k2, p1.
Row 5-10: Repeat rows 3-4 three times.
Row 11: Sl1 kwise wyib, k2, place marker, *k2, k2tog, k2, [k2tog] seven times, k3, k2tog, k2, place marker; repeat from * to last 3 stitches, k2, p1. (114 [132] stitches - 18 between each set of markers (six repeats for S/M, seven repeats for M/L, plus 3 stitches on each edge)
Row 12: Sl1 kwise wyib, k2, purl to last 3 stitches slipping markers as you go, k2, p1.

*Scarlett's Feather and Fan Chart*

| 4 | V | ● | ● | ● | ● | ● | ● | ● | ● | ● | ● | ● | ● | ● | ● | ● | ● | ● | ● | ● | ● | ● | ● |  |  |
|---|---|---|---|---|---|---|---|---|---|---|---|---|---|---|---|---|---|---|---|---|---|---|---|---|---|
|  | ● |  |  | / | / | / |  | O |  | O |  | O |  | O |  | O |  | O | / | / | / |  |  | V | 3 |
| 2 | V | ● | ● |  |  |  |  |  |  |  |  |  |  |  |  |  |  |  |  |  |  | ● | ● |  |  |
|  | ● |  |  |  |  |  |  |  |  |  |  |  |  |  |  |  |  |  |  |  |  |  |  | V | 1 |

V slip stitch kwise wyib
/ k2tog
(blank) RS: knit; WS: purl
O yarnover
● RS: purl, WS: knit

## *Shopping List*

Maggi Knits *Maggi Linen* (52% cotton, 48% linen, 126 yards/115m); 1 skein each Green #31 and Yellow #22

Size US 8 (5mm) 24" (60cm) circular needle

Size US 6 (4mm) double pointed needles (set of 2)

Small piece of cardboard for winding tassels

Tapestry needle

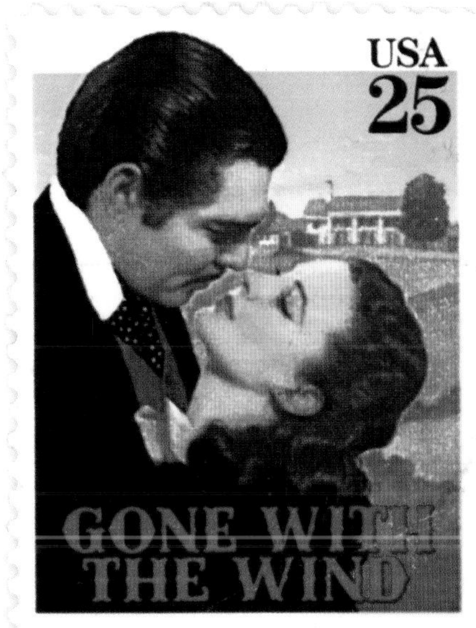

*Green lace section*
Cut Yellow yarn, leaving 8" (20cm) tail. Join Green.
Row 13: Sl1 kwise wyib, knit to last stitch, p1.
Row 14: Sl1 kwise wyib, knit to last stitch, p1.
Row 15-16: Repeat rows 13-14.
Row 17-40: Work 6 repeats of *Scarlett's Feather and Fan.*
Row 41: Sl1 kwise wyib, knit to last stitch, p1.
Row 42: Sl1 kwise wyib, k2, purl to last three stitches, k2, p1.
Row 43: Sl1 kwise wyib, k2, remove marker, k5, k2tog, k4, k2tog, k5, remove marker, *k2, [k2tog] seven times, k2, remove marker; repeat from * three [four] times more, k5, k2tog, k4, k2tog, k5, remove marker, k2, p1. (82 [93] stitches) Do not bind off. Cut yarn leaving 8" (20cm) tail.

## Finishing

*Tie*
With Yellow and double-pointed needles, CO 5 stitches, leaving 12" (30cm) tail.
Work 5 stitch I-cord for 12 (14)" [30 (36)cm].
*Begin I-cord bind off*
Work 4 stitches of next row of I-cord. With right side of fichu facing you, slip first live stitch of fichu to the double-pointed needle. Knit last stitch of I-cord together with slipped live stitch of the fichu. Continue working I-cord, knitting the last stitch of each I-cord row together with next live stitch from the fichu until all fichu stitches have been bound off in the I-cord. Continue working I-cord for 12 (14)" [30 (36)cm]. BO all I-cord stitches, leaving 8" (20cm) tail. Run the tail through BO stitches, pull tight and fasten. Repeat for tail at other end of the tie.

*Tassel ends (make 2)*
Cut a piece of cardboard 3" (7.5cm) high. Wrap Yellow yarn around the cardboard 20 times. Cut a 10" (25cm) length of yarn and slide under the wraps and up to top of cardboard; tie tightly. Slide the tied yarn from the cardboard. Cut a second 10" (25cm) piece of Yellow yarn and tie it around the tassels about 3/4" (2cm) from the top. Wrap the yarn around several times before knotting. Using the tails of the I-cord, stitch one tassel to each tie end. Using a tapestry needle, run the ends of top and side ties into the tassel. Trim the bottom ends even, cutting open the loops.

Weave in all ends. Wet thoroughly and block to finished size.

## Tips

- Though this lace pattern has a short row repeat and is a relatively simple lace pattern, because of the large number of stitches, use stitch markers between vertical repeats and use lifelines after every 4 row horizontal repeat, being careful not to run the lifeline through the stitch markers.
- Linen is a bit stiff and unforgiving while knitting it, but goes soft as flannel after washing and blocking.
- When working the I-cord bind off, make sure you give the first stitch a good tug once it's on the right hand needle. The yarn has zero spring and if you don't work the first stitch tightly, you'll have a floppy back side. Yeah, I know....
- This fichu, knit entirely in white or cream (with a beaded edge?) would make a lovely and very inexpensive addition to a summer bridal ensemble. It's quick enough to knit up color-coordinated pieces for the bridesmaids, too.

# Peach Cobbler

*Plump, juicy peaches are one of the joys of summer. This cobbler can be made with fresh peaches in season, or with canned fruit in the dead of winter. The slices are layered on top of an easy sweet batter that puffs up during baking and magically forms a buttery brown sugar cake. Served warm in a big bowl, this is my favorite winter breakfast. Don't judge— it has fruit.*

## Directions

*Tip*: If using fresh peaches, slice into a bowl, sprinkle with an extra 1/2 cup of granulated sugar and allow to stand at room temperature for one hour.

Preheat oven to 350 degrees.

Add melted butter to a 9"x13" pan. In a medium bowl, mix together flour, sugar, baking powder and salt. In a small bowl, beat together milk and the egg then add to the dry ingredients. Pour the batter over the melted butter in the pan. Do not stir.

In a large bowl, mix together the drained peaches, brown sugar, cinnamon and nutmeg. Layer the peach mixture over the batter, without stirring.

Bake 35-45 minutes or until the top is golden brown. As the cobbler bakes, the batter will rise to almost cover the peaches.

Serve warm with fresh sweetened whipped cream or real vanilla ice cream.

### Shopping List

1/2 cup melted butter

1 cup flour

1/2 cup granulated sugar

1/2 cup brown sugar

2 tsp baking powder

1/4 tsp salt

2/3 cup milk, room temperature

1 egg, room temperature

(1) 28oz can and (1) 15oz can of sliced peaches packed in fruit juice, drained

1 tsp cinnamon

1/2 tsp nutmeg

Extras

# About Sizing

For all the garments in the book, we provide the finished bust/chest sizes. However, since different designs are intended to be worn with specific amounts of ease, or room across the chest, we've provided "Fit Tips" in each garment pattern to help you choose your correct pattern size. Each pattern also tells you which size the model is wearing, so you can better gauge your fit.

**Patricia**
Height: 5'8" (1.73m)
Bust: 39" (99cm)
Standard size:
US Misses' 8 (UK 4)

**Elisha**
Height: 5'7" (1.7m)
Bust: 35" (89cm)
Standard size:
US Misses' 4-6 (UK 6-8)

**Olivia**
Height: 5'7" (1.7m)
Bust: 34" (86cm)
Standard size:
US Misses' 2-4 (UK 4-6)

**Cavan**
Height: 5'11" (1.8m)
Chest: 40" (107cm)
Standard size:
Men's 40 regular (UK 40)

# How-To Videos for this Book on PlanetPurl.com

**Cast Ons:**
Backward Loop Cast On
Knitted Cast On
Long Tail Cast On
Moebius Cast On
Provisional Cast On

**Bind Offs:**
Beaded Picot Bind Off
Bind Off in Knit
Bind Off in Pattern
Bind Off in Purl
I-Cord Bind Off
Three Needle Bind Off

**Knit and Purl:**
1x1 Rib
Drop Stitch
Garter Stitch
Knit Stitch (American and Continental)
Knit Through Back Loop
Knitting in the Round
Make Bobble
Pick Up and Knit
Purl Stitch
Seed Stitch
Short Row Shaping
Slip Stitch with Yarn in Back/Front
Stockinette and Reverse Stockinette

**Increases:**
Knit 1 Front & Back (k1f&b)
M1 Left Leaning
M1 Right Leaning
Yarnovers and Double Yarnovers

**Decreases:**
Knit 2 Together (k2tog)
Purl 2 Together (p2tog)
Ssk: slip, slip, knit decrease

**Lace Knitting:**
Blocking Lace
Knitting with Lifelines
Reading Lace Charts

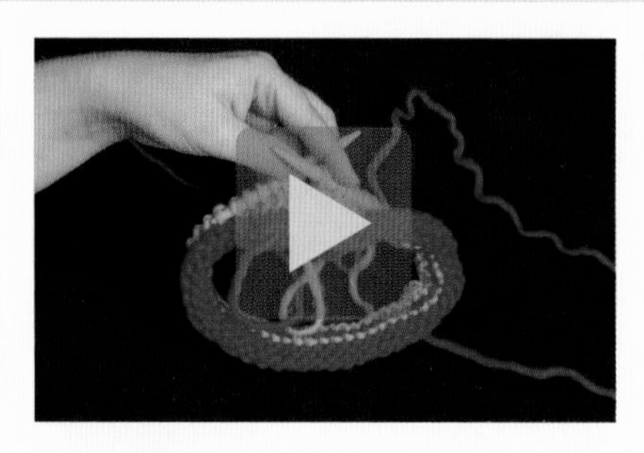

**Colorwork:**
Intarsia
Knitting Jogless Stripes in the Round
Making Yarn Butterflies (Bobbins)
Reading Color Charts
Stranded (Fair Isle) Knitting

**Lace Knitting:**
Blocking Lace
Knitting with Lifelines
Reading Lace Charts

**Finishing:**
Blanket Stitch
Duplicate Stitch Embroidery
Kitchener Stitch
Lining a Felted Bag
Mattress Stitch
Running Stitch
Sewing in a Zipper
Whipstitch

**Crochet:**
Crochet Chain
Double Crochet (Treble Crochet UK)
Half Double Crochet (Half Treble Crochet in UK)
Single Crochet (Double Crochet in UK)
Slip Stitch Crochet
Treble Crochet (Double Treble in UK)

**Free Online Classes:**
Beaded Knitting
Intarsia
Needle-Felting

# Abbreviations

**BO:** bind off
**CC:** contrast color (followed by # if more than one)
**Ch:** chain (crochet)
**Ch-space:** space between crochet stitches
**CO:** cast on
**Dc:** double crochet (treble crochet in UK)
**Hdc:** half double crochet (half treble crochet in UK)
**K:** knit
**k#tog:** knit designated number of stitches together
**K1f&b:** knit into front and back of same stitch
**K1tbl:** knit one stitch through the back loop
**Kwise:** as if to knit
**LH:** left hand
**M1:** make 1 increase
**MC:** main color
**P:** purl
**P#tog:** purl designated number of stitches together
**Pm:** place marker
**Pwise:** as if to purl
**RH:** right hand
**RS:** right side
**Sc:** single crochet (double crochet in UK)
**Sk:** skip (crochet)
**Sk2p:** slip 1 stitch, k2tog, pass slipped stitch over
**Sl :** slip stitch (crochet)
**Sl#:** slip specified number of stitches (knitting)
**Ssk:** slip, slip, knit decrease
**Trc:** treble crochet (double treble in UK)
**WS:** wrong side
**Wr&t:** wrap & turn for short row shaping
**Wyif:** with yarn in front
**Wyib:** with yarn in back
**Yo:** yarnover increase (yarn forward in UK)

# Basic Stitch Instructions

**Stockinette Stitch (worked back and forth):**
Row 1 (RS): Knit.
Row 2 (WS): Purl.

**Stockinette Stitch (worked in the round):**
All rounds: Knit.

**Garter Stitch (worked back and forth):**
All rows: Knit.

**Garter Stitch (worked in the round):**
Round 1: Knit.
Round 2: Purl.

**1x1 Rib (back and forth over even number of stitches):**
All rows: *K1, p1; repeat from * to end.

**1x1 Rib (back and forth over odd number of stitches):**
Row 1: K1, *p1, k1; repeat from * to end.
Row 2: P1, *k1, p1; repeat from * to end.
Repeat row 1-2 for pattern.

**1x1 Rib (in the round on an even number of stitches):**
Round 1: *K1, p1; repeat from * to end.
Round 2 and all subsequent rounds: Knit the knit stitches and purl the purl stitches.

**I-cord (on 2 double pointed needles):**
CO desired number of stitches. Knit across all stitches, but do not turn work at end of row. *Change needle with stitches to left hand, with working yarn to the back. Without turning the needle, push the just-knit stitches to the opposite end of the needle. Pull the working yarn up snug behind the stitches and knit across again, creating a hollow tube of knitting. Repeat from * for desired length. BO all stitches.

There are three parts to making sure your garments fit— choosing the right size, working at the specified gauge, and then blocking your pieces to the required dimensions before sewing them up. Here you can find charts with finished dimensions (in inches) of each piece for blocking.

### 1865 Jacket (*Page 10*)

| **Sizes:** | **XXS** | **XS** | **S** | **M** | **L** | **XL** | **1X** | **2X** |
|---|---|---|---|---|---|---|---|---|
| **Back** | | | | | | | | |
| *Length:* | | | | | | | | |
| Center back hem to center back neck | 24 1/8 | 24 1/2 | 24 1/2 | 25 | 25 1/2 | 25 1/2 | 25 3/4 | 25 3/4 |
| Bottom center hem to side (difference) | 1/2 | 1/2 | 1/2 | 1/2 | 1/2 | 1/2 | 1/2 | 1/2 |
| Side hem to armhole | 15 5/8 | 15 3/4 | 15 7/8 | 16 | 16 1/4 | 16 1/4 | 16 1/4 | 16 7/8 |
| Bottom of armhole to outside shoulder | 7 3/8 | 7 1/2 | 7 3/4 | 7 7/8 | 8 1/8 | 8 3/8 | 8 5/8 | 8 3/4 |
| Bottom of shoulder to top of shoulder | 7/8 | 1 | 1 1/8 | 1 1/4 | 1 1/4 | 1 1/4 | 1 3/8 | 1 3/8 |
| *Width:* | | | | | | | | |
| Hem edge | 20 3/8 | 21 1/8 | 21 3/4 | 22 3/8 | 23 1/4 | 24 1/8 | 25 | 25 3/4 |
| Waist | 16 3/4 | 17 5/8 | 18 | 18 3/4 | 19 5/8 | 20 3/4 | 21 5/8 | 22 3/4 |
| Below armhole shaping | 19 1/4 | 19 5/8 | 20 3/8 | 20 3/4 | 21 5/8 | 22 3/8 | 23 1/4 | 24 |
| Outside armhole to outside shoulder | 2 3/8 | 2 5/8 | 2 3/4 | 2 7/8 | 3 1/4 | 3 1/2 | 3 3/4 | 4 1/8 |
| Shoulder edge | 4 | 4 1/8 | 4 1/4 | 4 3/8 | 4 3/8 | 4 1/2 | 4 5/8 | 4 5/8 |
| Neck edge | 5 7/8 | 6 | 6 1/8 | 6 1/8 | 6 1/8 | 6 1/8 | 6 1/4 | 6 1/2 |
| **Front** | | | | | | | | |
| *Length:* | | | | | | | | |
| Center hem to bottom of neck shaping | 13 | 13 1/4 | 13 5/8 | 14 | 14 3/8 | 14 3/8 | 14 5/8 | 15 |
| Side hem to armhole | 15 3/8 | 15 7/8 | 15 7/8 | 16 | 16 3/4 | 16 5/8 | 16 1/4 | 16 7/8 |
| Bottom of armhole to outside shoulder | 7 3/8 | 7 1/2 | 7 3/4 | 7 7/8 | 8 1/8 | 8 3/8 | 8 5/8 | 8 3/4 |
| Bottom of shoulder to top of shoulder | 7/8 | 1 | 1 1/8 | 1 1/4 | 1 1/4 | 1 1/4 | 1 3/8 | 1 3/8 |
| Bottom neck opening to top shoulder | 11 1/4 | 11 3/8 | 11 1/2 | 11 3/4 | 11 7/8 | 11 7/8 | 12 1/8 | 12 1/4 |

## 1865 Jacket continued... (*Page 10*)

| Sizes: | XXS | XS | S | M | L | XL | 1X | 2X |
|---|---|---|---|---|---|---|---|---|
| **Front, continued** | | | | | | | | |
| *Width:* | | | | | | | | |
| Hem edge | 10 1/4 | 10 5/8 | 10 7/8 | 11 1/8 | 11 5/8 | 12 | 12 1/2 | 12 7/8 |
| Waist | 8 3/8 | 8 3/4 | 9 | 9 3/8 | 9 3/4 | 10 3/8 | 10 3/4 | 11 3/8 |
| At bottom of neck shaping | 9 1/4 | 9 3/8 | 9 3/4 | 10 | 10 3/4 | 11 | 11 3/8 | 12 |
| Below armhole shaping | 8 3/8 | 8 3/4 | 9 | 9 3/8 | 10 | 10 1/4 | 10 3/4 | 11 1/4 |
| From center front to inside shoulder | 3 | 3 | 3 | 3 | 3 1/8 | 3 1/8 | 3 1/4 | 3 1/4 |
| Outside armhole to outside shoulder | 2 3/8 | 2 5/8 | 2 3/4 | 2 7/8 | 3 1/4 | 3 1/2 | 3 3/4 | 4 1/8 |
| Shoulder edge | 4 | 4 1/8 | 4 1/4 | 4 3/8 | 4 3/8 | 4 1/2 | 4 5/8 | 4 5/8 |
| **Sleeves** | | | | | | | | |
| *Length:* | | | | | | | | |
| CO edge to top of scoop | 4 1/8 | 4 1/8 | 4 1/8 | 4 1/8 | 4 1/8 | 4 1/8 | 4 1/8 | 4 1/8 |
| Bottom center hem to bottom of cap | 13 1/2 | 13 1/2 | 13 1/2 | 13 1/2 | 13 5/8 | 13 7/8 | 14 1/8 | 14 1/8 |
| Bottom of cap to top of cap | 5 3/4 | 5 7/8 | 6 3/8 | 6 1/2 | 6 1/2 | 6 5/8 | 6 5/8 | 7 |
| Center hem to top of cap | 19 1/4 | 19 3/8 | 19 7/8 | 20 | 20 1/8 | 20 1/2 | 20 3/4 | 21 1/8 |
| *Width:* | | | | | | | | |
| At top of hem scoop | 11 1/4 | 12 | 12 3/8 | 12 3/8 | 12 3/4 | 13 | 13 3/8 | 13 3/8 |
| At bottom of cap | 12 3/4 | 13 5/8 | 14 | 14 | 14 3/8 | 14 5/8 | 15 3/8 | 15 3/8 |
| At top of cap | 2 3/4 | 3 1/4 | 3 1/4 | 3 1/4 | 3 1/4 | 3 3/8 | 3 3/4 | 3 3/4 |

## Camellia Baby Set (*Page 86*)

| Measurements | Width at eyelet row | Width at chest | Height from drawstring |
|---|---|---|---|
| **Back** | 20 | 13 1/4 | 23 |
| **Front** | 10 3/8 | 7 1/4 | 23 |
| | **Width** | **Total length** | |
| **Sleeve** | 10 1/2 | 8 1/4 | |

## Cherokee Vest (*Page 102*)

| **Sizes:** | **S** | **M** | **L** |
|---|---|---|---|
| **Back** | | | |
| *Length:* | | | |
| Hem to top of shoulder | 19 | 19 1/2 | 20 |
| Hem to bottom of armhole | 12 3/4 | 13 1/4 | 13 3/4 |
| Bottom of armhole to shoulder | 6 1/4 | 6 1/4 | 6 1/4 |
| *Width:* | | | |
| Below armhole edging | 17 | 20 | 23 |
| Shoulder after edging | 7 | 7 1/4 | 7 1/2 |
| Hem | 19 5/8 | 23 | 26 1/2 |
| **Front** | | | |
| Front is laid flat over the back to block, with gap width: | 0 | 1 1/2 | 3 1/2 |

## Dogwood Cardigan (*Page 42*)

| **Sizes:** | **S** | **M** | **L** |
|---|---|---|---|
| **Back** | | | |
| *Length:* | | | |
| Hem to beginning of Citrus stockinette | 8 5/8 | 8 5/8 | 8 5/8 |
| Citrus stockinette to armholes | 7 | 8 | 8 |
| From armhole to shoulder shaping | 8 | 8 5/8 | 9 |
| Hem to shoulder shaping | 23 5/8 | 25 1/4 | 25 5/8 |
| *Width:* | | | |
| Hem | 24 1/2 | 26 1/2 | 28 1/2 |
| Below armhole shaping | 19 1/2 | 20 7/8 | 22 1/4 |
| **Front** | | | |
| *Length:* | | | |
| Hem to beginning of Citrus stockinette | 8 5/8 | 8 5/8 | 8 5/8 |
| Citrus stockinette to armholes | 7 | 8 | 8 |
| Hem to neck shaping | 8 | 9 1/2 | 9 1/2 |
| From armhole to shoulder shaping | 8 | 8 5/8 | 9 |
| Hem to shoulder shaping | 23 5/8 | 25 1/4 | 25 5/8 |

## Dogwood Cardigan continued... (*Page 42*)

| Sizes: | S | M | L |
|---|---|---|---|
| **Front, continued** | | | |
| *Width:* | | | |
| Hem | 12 1/2 | 14 1/2 | 16 1/2 |
| Below armhole shaping | 9 3/8 | 10 5/8 | 12 |
| **Sleeves** | | | |
| *Length:* | | | |
| Hem to bottom of cap | 11 | 12 | 13 |
| Bottom to top of cap | 2 3/4 | 3 1/8 | 4 |
| Hem to top of cap | 13 3/4 | 15 1/8 | 17 |
| *Width:* | | | |
| Hem | 14 1/2 | 14 1/2 | 15 |
| Below armhole shaping | 14 5/8 | 15 1/2 | 16 1/2 |

## Ozark Vest (*Page 52*)

| Sizes: | XS | S | M | L | XL | 1X | 2X | 3X |
|---|---|---|---|---|---|---|---|---|
| **Back/Front** | | | | | | | | |
| *Length:* | | | | | | | | |
| Hem to armhole | 14 5/8 | 14 1/2 | 14 5/8 | 14 3/8 | 14 1/2 | 14 3/8 | 14 1/4 | 14 |
| Armhole to outside of shoulder | 9 1/2 | 9 5/8 | 9 7/8 | 10 | 10 1/4 | 10 3/8 | 10 5/8 | 10 3/4 |
| Outside shoulder to top of shoulder | 1 1/8 | 1 1/4 | 1 1/4 | 1 3/8 | 1 3/8 | 1 1/2 | 1 5/8 | 1 3/4 |
| *Width:* | | | | | | | | |
| Body (above ribbing) | 21 1/8 | 22 1/4 | 23 3/8 | 24 1/2 | 25 5/8 | 26 3/4 | 27 7/8 | 29 1/8 |
| Outside armhole to outside shoulder edge | 2 1/2 | 2 7/8 | 3 1/8 | 3 5/8 | 4 1/8 | 4 3/8 | 4 7/8 | 5 1/4 |
| Outside shoulder to inside shoulder | 4 1/2 | 4 5/8 | 4 3/4 | 4 7/8 | 5 | 5 1/8 | 5 1/4 | 5 1/4 |
| **Back Only** | | | | | | | | |
| *Width:* Neck edge | 7 | 7 1/4 | 7 1/2 | 7 5/8 | 7 5/8 | 7 5/8 | 7 3/4 | 8 1/8 |
| **Front Only** | | | | | | | | |
| *Length:* Bottom of v-neck to top of shoulder | 7 3/4 | 7 7/8 | 8 | 8 | 8 | 8 | 8 1/8 | 8 1/4 |

## Lighthouse Tunic (*Page 136*)

| **Sizes:** | **S** | **M** | **L** | **XL** |
|---|---|---|---|---|
| **Back/Front** | | | | |
| *Length:* | | | | |
| Hem to top of shoulder | 31 1/8 | 32 1/8 | 32 7/8 | 33 5/8 |
| Hem to bottom of armhole | 21 3/4 | 22 1/4 | 22 1/2 | 22 7/8 |
| Bottom of armhole to outside of shoulder | 9 | 9 1/2 | 10 | 10 3/8 |
| Outside shoulder to inside shoulder edge | 3/8 | 3/8 | 3/8 | 3/8 |
| *Width:* | | | | |
| Hem (above ribbing) | 23 1/4 | 24 3/8 | 25 1/2 | 27 1/4 |
| Outside hem edge to outside shoulder edge | 6 1/2 | 7 | 7 5/8 | 8 1/4 |
| Width of shoulder strap (other then rib) | 1 1/2 | 1 5/8 | 1 3/4 | 1 3/4 |
| **Back Only** | | | | |
| *Length:* Base of neck to top of shoulder | 1 | 1 | 1 | 1 |
| *Width:* Neck edge not including rib | 6 1/2 | 6 5/8 | 6 3/4 | 7 1/8 |
| **Front Only** | | | | |
| *Length:* Scoop neck (before rib) to top of shoulder | 7 | 7 1/8 | 7 1/4 | 7 1/2 |
| *Width:* Inside neck edge (not including rib) | 6 1/2 | 6 5/8 | 6 3/4 | 7 1/8 |

## Sunshine Sweater (*Page 62*)

| **Sizes:** | **S** | **M** | **L** | **XL** |
|---|---|---|---|---|
| **Back/Front** | | | | |
| *Length:* | | | | |
| Hem to top of shoulder (before saddle) | 17 | 17 1/2 | 18 1/2 | 19 1/2 |
| Hem to bottom of armhole | 10 1/2 | 11 | 12 | 13 |
| Armhole to shoulder (before saddle) | 6 1/2 | 6 1/2 | 6 1/2 | 6 1/2 |
| *Width:* | | | | |
| Hem (side to side) | 17 1/2 | 19 | 20 3/4 | 22 1/2 |
| Bust at bottom of armhole | 17 1/2 | 19 | 20 3/4 | 22 1/2 |
| Width of shoulder edge/saddle | 3 | 3 1/2 | 3 3/4 | 4 |
| **Saddles** | | | | |
| *Length:* | 2 | 2 5/8 | 2 5/8 | 3 |
| *Width:* | 3 | 3 1/2 | 3 3/4 | 4 |
| **Sleeves** | | | | |
| *Length:* | 5 7/8 | 6 3/8 | 6 7/8 | 7 3/8 |

## Treasure Coast Tennis Vest (*Page 122*)

| **Sizes:** | **S** | **M** | **L** |
|---|---|---|---|
| **Back/Front** | | | |
| *Length:* | | | |
| Hem to bottom of armhole | 13 | 13 1/2 | 14 |
| Armhole to outside edge of shoulder | 6 1/2 | 6 1/2 | 6 1/2 |
| Hem to outside edge of shoulder | 6 3/4 | 7 | 7 |
| *Width:* | | | |
| Hem and bust (side to side) | 16 7/8 | 19 1/4 | 20 7/8 |
| Shoulder width (before edging) | 2 1/4 | 2 3/8 | 2 5/8 |
| **Back Only** | | | |
| *Width:* neck edge | 6 3/8 | 7 1/4 | 7 5/8 |
| **Front Only** | | | |
| *Length:* hem to bottom of v-neck | 11 5/8 | 12 1/8 | 12 5/8 |

# Index

## Notes

# Notes